THE DIGITAL NOMAD BLUEPRINT

How to Become a Digital Nomad

By Salvador Briggman

Table of Contents

INTRODUCTION

This book is about you. It's about your future, your potential, and what you want to do with your life.

World travel is a relatively new concept. In our parent's generation, travel consisted of visiting local states, cities, and maybe an occasional cruise or vacation abroad. It was rare, and virtually unheard of, for someone to travel the world, work from their laptop, and hang out with others who are doing the same.

It wasn't until 1997 that the term "digital nomad" entered the English language. It took a few more years for this career option to gain awareness in the mainstream culture with Tim Ferriss' 2007 book, The Four-Hour Work week. Still, I would argue, that it wasn't until 2013 that I actually began to witness people travel the world, work out of coworking spaces, and use websites like Airbnb to find cheap housing throughout their trek.

Now, you have the entire planet at your fingertips. You can spend months abroad, exploring the third world, or living large in ritzy apartments that are affordable due to a term known as "geoarbitrage." This is when you move to a place with a lower cost of living but continue to earn the same level of income from your online work. It's all possible because of the internet! This is the best time to be alive.

Over time, a proven path has emerged to introduce newcomers to the digital nomad lifestyle. The territory has already been plotted out. I can share with you exactly how to earn income online, where to find the best digital nomad spots, and how to integrate seamlessly into the lifestyle. You just have to follow the road map that I'll lay out in the coming pages. If you're looking to design your own life, then you're on the right track.

I've been location-independent since 2012 and I began my own digital nomad travels in 2015. I moved to NYC after finishing school at George Washington Uni (in Washington DC). As much as I loved the city, I became enthralled with the idea of traveling to far off destinations that I'd only seen in movies. I had been working from home for a few years before I finally built up the courage to try it out. It was my first time traveling alone. I visited Thailand for a month to get my bearings. The goal was to figure out whether or not this lifestyle was for me.

I remember the moment that I stepped foot on Karon beach in Phuket, Thailand. The sand was a gentle creamy white, leading towards a crystal-clear turquoise ocean. I walked towards the shoreline, taking in the breathtaking view. Without a second thought, I plunged into the warm water and paddled further and further, until I was up to my chest. The waves gently tumbled towards me, taking their leisurely time to reach to shore. "This is life," I thought to myself. This is where it's at. Humans weren't meant to live in big office buildings and cramped apartments. We are supposed to be in nature, just like this. With that thought, I dove into the water and let the coolness surround my entire body. Right then, there was nowhere else I wanted to be.

Since my first trip, I've been to El Salvador, Colombia, Peru, Spain, Cambodia, Vietnam, and The Philippines. I've also been back to Thailand a few times. Along the way, I've met some incredible people, seen beautiful majestic sights, and come to grow spiritually, emotionally, and professionally. I've learned a tremendous amount about being a digital nomad and in this book, I want to pass that on to you.

This is the real deal. I've broken the entire process down into what I refer to as "ILL." That means:

- **Income:** How do you earn income in a location-independent fashion so that you can fuel the digital nomad lifestyle?

- **Location:** What are the best locations for digital nomads? What should you keep in mind when choosing a great location?

- **Lifestyle:** How do you prepare for this lifestyle shift? What should you know before taking the plunge? How do you deal with common problems like finding friends, dealing with depression, and balancing your time?

Throughout this book, we will examine each of these. Along with providing my own findings, I'll also connect you with tried and true resources to help you along this path. You'll go from feeling anxious, nervous, and uncertain to confident, excited, and ready to book your plane ticket!

By now, I'm sure you've seen other digital nomads who are living out the lifestyle. You know that it's possible. You're just missing the "how to." There are a few missing pieces of the puzzle, and you're wondering how they fit together. Things like taxes, visas, living spaces, and even the legality of being a digital nomad. You'll get answers to all of your questions in this book.

As you go through each page, you'll gain more clarity and insight into the digital nomad lifestyle. I've also tailored this book to a few different types of individuals, meaning that no matter what your background is, what your skillset is, or where you're from, you're gonna get some real value out of it! Chances are, there is someone just like you who's traveling the world as we speak. The only difference between them and you is this "know-how."

I'm excited for you to start this journey! You're about to take the first step towards the future you've always wanted. How freakin' awesome is that!? I hope that you enjoy the hard work that I've put into making this content available for you. If you have any questions, you can reach out to me online or on one of my social media profiles. I will do my best to help you out.

- Salvador Briggman

CHAPTER 1:

Digital Nomad vs. Location Independent - What's the Difference?

There actually **IS** a difference between a digital nomad and a location-independent entrepreneur or freelancer. I've been both at various times in my life. There are advantages and disadvantages that come with each.

I want to get into the nitty gritty of not only what these are, but how they relate to you. What does it mean for you in your quest for more freedom, happiness, and flexibility in your life? Is one better for you than another? We'll get to the bottom of this so that you can make the best choices going forward. Are you ready for a little logic puzzle? (actually – I hate puzzles)

All digital nomads are location independent individuals, but not all location independent workers are digital nomads.

Whaaa!?!?

Yeah, that kind of messed with my head when I first heard that concept. Let me wipe away the confusion and break that down for you.

<u>What is a Digital Nomad?</u>

A digital nomad is someone who earns income from their laptop. That's where the word "digital" comes from in the phrase. They use their computer and WIFI connection to earn money online. There are many ways to go about doing this.

Sometimes, a digital nomad is a business owner, but not always. I've met many digital nomads in my travelers who are freelancers, or who work for a company that gives them the flexibility to travel. I am a business owner.

I recently went to Medellin, Colombia on my digital nomad travels. I was working from my laptop doing things like producing podcast episodes, making YouTube videos, and writing content for my blog. Right off the bat, you'll notice that one of the major elements of being a digital nomad is…. travel! That's the second part of the popular phrase. As a nomad, you're traveling from place to place as you work. You could spend a couple of months in a location or only a few weeks. However, you're probably not spending a few years, otherwise you're crossing over into expat territory.

Over the course of seven months, I also visited countries like Peru, Spain, Thailand, Cambodia, Vietnam, and the Philippines. I was bouncing all over the globe, but typically, it's more common to spend time in one region of the world, like South East Asia. The reason I was able to do this is that, as a nomad, I can earn income online so all I need is a WIFI connection to keep everything flowing behind the scenes. There are many types of businesses that let you do this.

Travel is an important distinction because it defines your lifestyle. It almost becomes a bit of a part-time job, quite frankly. You have to figure out where you want to travel, what the visa requirements are, what there is to do, and also what activities you're going to participate in to meet other travelers.

As a digital nomad you will:

- Need to book Airbnbs on a regular basis (or hotel/hostels)

- Figure out your travel itinerary and next destinations

- Book flights regularly to new places

- Decide on the fun activities you want to do

- Keep an eye on international news

- Be aware of how visa requirements work.

- Learn how to pack lean and light

Like I said, you become a mini expert in travel itself. You'll learn how to plan trip itineraries, find cool stuff to do, and which countries are most friendly for digital nomads. A lot of beginners underestimate the sheer level of research and planning that goes into this. If you don't have a travel agent, then you basically have to take on their job!

Most importantly, you'll want to get a firm grasp of visa laws, which countries you want to visit, and when you'll want to book your tickets. Throughout my travels, I used Airbnb as the main way to find places to stay, though I also stayed at hostels sometimes.

The Digital Nomad Lifestyle

The most important thing I can tell you is that being a digital nomad is not the same thing as taking a vacation! You will be working, as you would in a regular job. For the average person out there, that means 40 hours per week. You'll have to either work from home or from a co-working space.

I never had an issue finding a coworking space when I was traveling, even when I was Latin America. The concept of coworking is really starting to spread across the globe. In the worst case, you might have to work out of a cafe. You'll probably notice the one with the best WIFI based on the sea of laptops that you see when you go there.

You can meet people at these coworking spaces after work, or you can participate in fun activities. I did some cool stuff like, Muay Thai, when I was in Thailand. Haha – it's a lot harder than it looks, but it was so much fun!

This is an activity that I never considered trying out in my home country, but it was relatively cheap in Thailand, and I wanted to get outside of my comfort zone. Simply by being in a new location can make you expand your horizons and try out new things.

Unlike in the United States, there are lots of easy day trips where you can go from one climate to another. For example, when I was in the city of Bangkok, I decided that I wanted to go to the beach for the weekend. So, I got on a plane and went to Krabi. You could get a plane to other places like Phuket, for not terribly much money. It was a weekend of bliss chilling in the sun and eating healthy food.

You can very easily go from island to island if you'd like and do fun activities like kayaking, snorkeling, or paddle boarding. If you're in the stage of your life where you want to travel, have spiritual experiences, meet new people, and discover new locations, then being a digital nomad is right for you! There are also many couples who travel together as nomads and even families! The main difference between a digital nomad and someone who is simply location-independent is that *consistent travel* is associated with being a nomad.

What is a Location-Independent Individual?

A location independent entrepreneur or worker typically earns income from their laptop also. They might be a freelancer, work-at-home employee, or a business owner. The big difference is that they don't always travel. They may be in one location for their entire life, or only decide to travel when going on vacation. They don't make travel a part of their lifestyle.

I also fall into this category! For many years of my life after college (6 years) I was living in New York City in an expensive studio apartment in Williamsburg, Brooklyn. I still live in New York and enjoy the city, but during this this post-college 6-year phase of my life, I wasn't really traveling much at all. If I was, it was because I was on vacation.

During this time, I was able to earn money from my laptop, but I wasn't doing any traveling. So, I was location-independent, but I mainly worked at home, at cafes, or at a local coworking space in Brooklyn called The Yard. I also worked out of one in Williamsburg called Kettle Space.

<u>This is how I was earning my income:</u>

- Blogging

- Podcasting

- YouTube

- Books & eBooks

- Affiliate marketing

- Advertising and sponsorships

- Online Courses

- Coaching Programs

I had built up those income streams since 2012. It happened over a number of years. It wasn't like they all came into being overnight. Now... the big difference, as I stated before, between a digital nomad and a location independent worker is the lifestyle. And.... I gotta be honest with you.

I was **WAY** more productive when I wasn't traveling.

Here's why.

Stability and routine, as boring as it is, is linked with productivity. When you have a lot of instability in terms of where you're staying and where you're going, then it's harder to have a normal routine. In addition, when you're traveling you have to account for time zones. You may have clients in very different time zones than you, so it can be hard to coordinate your work.

<u>Pros of being only location-independent:</u>

- Stability translates to **_productivity_**

- A regular schedule makes it easy to form lasting relationships.

- Being in one place makes you feel "more at home"

- You can still hang out with **_long-term friends_**

- You don't have to worry as much about bouncing around time zones.

<u>What is the lifestyle like?</u>

It's the work from home life!

You'll be working either at a coworking space, a cafe, or from home. Depending on the type of work I'd have to do, I would bounce between each of these. You'll be spending much more time exploring your local area. After work, I could go into New York City for cool events, to see a play, or to hang out with friends. I would also go to parks, go kayaking, and on nice scenic bike rides.

On the weekends, I would do fun things outside of the city, as long as they were in driving distance. I'd drive down with friends to the beach at Atlantic City, or go hiking in Upstate, New York. One time, I went to the Poconos, PA to go skydiving. It was so much fun!

Some of my fondest memories are those typical "New York moments," like seducing a pretty girl at a rooftop bar in the shadow of the Empire State Building, dancing the night away on a party boat traveling around Manhattan, or riding some pretty badass Jet Skis on the East River.

So, I wouldn't say there's terribly much difference between a location independent career and a normal one when it comes to the off-work hours. Just like a normal career, you can do what you want on your off time. The main difference between a location-independent career and a normal one is the discipline required to be able to work from home.

You have to know your working style, what environments make you the most productive, and how to make the best use of your time. You need to be a little more self-directed.

<u>You might be a better fit for this lifestyle if:</u>

- You're in a long-term relationship and can't travel

- You want to put your head down and be super productive

- You enjoy the city or place where you live.

Every once in a while, you can take a vacation and travel to far off destinations. It just won't be as much a part of your regular lifestyle.

This book will show you how to become a digital nomad, but if you follow my steps, you will also become location independent. Your career is the source of your income, and thus will fuel all of your travels. It's the foundation that can grant you the lifestyle of your dreams. To help simplify the rest of this book, I've broken this entire system down into three major components:

- I: Income independence – earn income anywhere.

- L: Location selection – choose the best digital nomad hub for your needs.

- L: Lifestyle mastery – knowing how to make friends, safeguard your health, and more.

You'll gain profound clarity once you get your hands on these teachings, which I deliver in an easy-to-digest bite-sized manner in the following chapters. As you move through this book, keep in mind the three pillars of becoming a digital nomad. They will help to simplify some of the valuable information that I'm going to throw your way.

CHAPTER 2:

What Digital Nomads Do For Work

Becoming a digital nomad used to be a pipe dream, now people are doing it at record rates. Research shows that there are 4.8 million digital nomads worldwide, and that trend is only growing. Location independent entrepreneurs and workers are traveling the globe, working from their laptop, and taking some pretty cool Instagram pics while doing it.

It's no longer some kind of "make money online" scheme that it used to be. There is a practical and proven path for achieving location independence in a matter of months. There is a cottage industry of websites, resources, and experts to show you how.

Whether you want to travel and see the world, are tired of working from a corporate cubical, or you just want to explore an alternative career path, there's nothing stopping you from claiming your freedom!

In this chapter, I want to go through what digital nomads actually do for work. We'll cover some of the pros and cons of location independent jobs, along with what you should know if you wanna take the leap. This is the gateway to a lifestyle of freedom, independence, and flexibility. Let's make sure you don't sacrifice your paycheck or your savings while you're trying to get there.

This time next year, if you follow my advice, you'll be chilling on a beach in Thailand, or looking at a majestic sunset in the Philippines.

Common "Things" Digital Nomads Do For Work

Location independent workers take advantage of what's called geo-arbitrage. They earn money in their home country's currency, while spending money in their local currency. Typically, the countries they are traveling through have a lower cost of living than they experience at home. For example, eating out might cost $30 (with tip + drinks) at home, but only $5 in a foreign country. Thus, your expenses would be far lower when abroad.

Think of this as earning a New York City level salary but being able to live in a rural place like Mississippi, where the median household income is only $43,441. In Manhattan, you gotta make at least $85k - $100k before life starts to resemble normal. Before that point, you probably are living with roommates in a not so great section of the city. You're basically paying a ridiculously high cost of living just to be in the center of all the activity. However, in Mississippi, you could live like a king on $100k per year. The living costs aren't nearly as high.

This same principle applies to the concept known as "geoarbitrage." In other words, your dollar goes a lot farther overseas than at home. Because of this simple fact, nomads don't have to earn as much money in order to enjoy the same lifestyle they had at home. Keep this in mind as you go through the next chapters of this book.

Now, let's get into some of the common fields for a location independent career. I'm going to breeze over some of these, just to give you a big picture of the career field, and then we can get a bit more in-depth later.

Writers, Editors, and Content Creators

It's no surprise that writers, editors, and online content creators make up a bulk of the jobs for digital nomads. All you really need to perform this kind of work is your laptop, an internet connection, and a client who values your work.

This is one of the reasons why so many bloggers become digital nomads. It's an easy transition if you already have some traffic and are monetizing it the right way. In addition, you can diversify your passive income by doing things like freelance writing for other businesses and blogs. Writing content online takes the form of what's called "content marketing," where you're helping a company develop educational materials for prospective clients. Those materials could be things like blog posts, but also be white papers, ebooks, guides, infographics, and more.

Designers, Artists, and Creative Types

Working with a variety of clients, design is also a common career path for digital nomads. Designers can work remotely, only needing the right software to get the job done. This fits well with working on the go. If you need to work in a quiet environment, you can always join a coworking space.

While freelancers make up the bulk of this career path, designers and artists can also earn passive income through the creation of website themes, royalty-free images, and other designs that can be sold on websites like ThemeForest.

IT Professionals (Programmers, Developers, etc)

If you have coding skills, or the ability to help develop valuable projects like apps, websites, and other tools, then your work will lend very well to the digital nomad lifestyle. You can work remotely with a team of individuals from a coworking space.

Good programmers are in such high demand that they rarely have trouble finding work. This gives them more choice and flexibility when it comes to where they want to work. Their existing company may even be willing to keep them on and allow them to work remotely.

Marketing and Online Communication

Social media marketing is booming! Every company now needs a social media presence, only most business owners don't have a clue as to what they're doing. They need help, and you can be there to hold their hand.

As a marketing professional, you'll need to learn a bit about organic marketing, paid marketing, and how to use social media tools, but once you do, this field is ripe for opportunity. You can become a valuable asset in a business by helping them to get traffic and convert that traffic into customers.

<u>Ecommerce</u>

Now a days with powerful business models like white labeling and drop shipping, it's easier than ever before to earn an income by selling products online through Amazon or your own website. You can also design and create your own product. You can even use crowdfunding to raise money for it!

The ecommerce industry is only going to grow in the next couple of years, and if you have a handle on the right product to sell, how to get traffic, and how to figure out your supply chain, you can easily operate your business while you're traveling the world.

<u>Teaching Online</u>

What I LOVE about teaching is that it can be combined with many of the above skillsets. For example, if you are a great writer, then you can also teach other people how to write. If you are a good designer, you can teach other designers how to design.

While it will require some upfront effort, teaching can be an incredibly effective way to begin to develop a new revenue stream for your business. It's also incredibly rewarding. You'll need to master a few basic things like marketing, video creation, and how to sell your courses, but once you do, it's off to the races!

Podcasting

A few years ago, I wouldn't have included Podcasting in this list, but in my recent travels abroad, I've met more and more nomads who are also podcasters. There is a good reason too!

Podcasting is confined to audio, so you don't have to worry as much about WIFI uploading speeds, or deal with the intensive editing that goes into video creation. You can record a show from anywhere, schedule it to go out at a later time, and just like with blogging, it's seeing a big surge in growth. Starting a podcast is a great way to get started building an audience online.

Online Video Work

Video editing can be done anywhere. I have editors from around the world who help me come out with new YouTube videos for my channel. As long as they get the job done, it doesn't matter to me what their location is.

You can start a career as a video editor for commercials, educational videos, explainer vids, or you can start your own YouTube channel and begin to build your brand. It's not that hard to earn some extra income doing just that.

Like with blogging or podcasting, you can also combine this with other forms of income-creation like affiliate marketing, online courses, books, etc. Now that we've gotten into some of the skills you can use, let's talk a bit about the actual career path.

You're an adult. You're not looking to make a little extra cash here and there. You're looking for a real, sustainable, career path with potential for growth. ***Right?***

Let's get into what this career path could look for the average person, even if you don't have any skills, experience, or previous history in the online world. Remember, a good chunk of nomads are actually over the age of 38!

The Digital Nomad Career Path – 5 Simple Steps

The question is simple.

How do you want to earn income?

Do you want to *trade* time for money?

Do you want to earn *passive* income?

Do you want to work for someone else or be *your own* boss?

Pick One... Employee or a Business Owner

As an employee, you could negotiate with your existing employer to see if they would be willing to let you work remotely for your full-time job. If not, they might be willing to keep you on for some part-time work if you're good at what you do. This can really help to supplement your income stream as you're searching for more work.

Freelancers also fall into the category of employee, though technically they are independent contractors. Rather than having one boss, they have multiple. They are selling their time for money and working from project to project. Becoming a freelancer is the easiest transition if you're not very familiar with online work. You can go on websites like Upwork to get started. I'll lay out a step-by-step process for getting work as a freelancing a bit later.

As a business owner, the type of business you choose will determine your viability for location independence. For example, owning a retail outlet in your city isn't going to give you any kind of flexibility. You'll have to deal with the daily management of your employees. It confines you to that location. It's kind of like a form of handcuffs.

Personally, I started my career as a blogger, transitioned into podcasting, and then into YouTube. I also sell books, digital courses, and do online coaching. My type of business is an "expert style" business, where I'm monetizing my skillset in a few different ways. There are lots and lots of profitable business ideas that we'll get into in future chapters.

Find a Good Training Program

I know, I know. Online training might seem "scammy" or it's weird to do something like take an online course. Right?

Well... take a step back. Anytime you were serious about a career path in life, chances are, you got a little bit educated about it. Maybe you went to college, so that you could earn more money at your job. Maybe you got an MBA so you could understand business and make a higher salary.

You could spend a little bit of time hunting around on YouTube or poking around on Google, but it will REALLY help if you enroll in a dedicated step-by-step program that shows you exactly how to become a digital nomad. There are some good ones out there. I also have an affordable and comprehensive course that I can tell you about towards the end of this book.

If you don't check out my own course, make sure that the one you enroll in covers a few things, including:

- *Tax implications* and regulations that you should be aware of

- The best and *fastest* ways to generate income

- The top *digital nomad hubs* and locations around the world

- Dealing with emotional issues like *loneliness* and fear

A good program should not only prep you for the lifestyle and the ways you can earn income, but also go through some of the great locations out there and cover some of the negative sides of the lifestyle, like loneliness. This book will help to answer many of your questions, but a real training program will hold you by the hand through this entire complicated process.

Gather Proof, Promises, and Results

If you do NOTHING else regarding the marketing of your personal brand, then at least develop proof, promises and results. As an employee, you likely had a resume. When it comes to online work, your resume doesn't matter as much. What's more important is the projects you've worked on.

- **Proof:** What proof do you have you did a good job in the past? Do you have testimonials? Awards? Media mentions?

- **Promises:** What can you do for other people? Example: *"I write an epic in-depth blog post to catch the eye of potentially lucrative customers."*

- **Results:** From a quantitative perspective, what have you done for others. Example: *"I wrote blog posts that drove 50k unique visitors to my client's blog over the course of a year."*

This is a very simple and doable format for getting clients or customers. The more that you work on your "case file," or the real reason why someone should give you money, then the sooner you'll start to make it.

I call this stacking ammo. Filling the war chest. This is valuable stuff, and your time gathering it is well spent.

Decide On Your TMI – Target Monthly Income

NO – This is NOT the same as your salary.

There are many factors that go into your existing salary that your employer is paying. As a nomad, you have to think about things like health care, taxes, standard of living differences, and travel costs. Your target monthly income may be lower or higher than what you anticipate. It all depends on the lifestyle you wanna have.

Your TMI will guide the choices you make going forward. Some people might say "well, I wanna make as much as possible." Realistically, you don't.

Here's why.

In order to make as much money as possible, you have to be WORKING as many hours as possible. Everyone wants to earn six or seven figures, but no one wants to work 80-hour weeks and give up having fun as you travel. I did this for the first 2 months of my last travel experience, and boy oh boy, it sucked. I was much happier when I had a stable balance of both work and fun.

Do This Before You Take The Leap

I strongly recommend that you do something before you become a full-time digital nomad and travel the world for the next 4 years.

I'd recommend that you do a mini-nomad experience, where you travel for a defined length of time, like 2 months, and see how it goes. Not everyone enjoys the digital nomad lifestyle. I did my first "Four Hour Work Week" experience in Thailand when I was 23.

Before you really take the leap, I'd do a trial run. Even if that's just a month of travel. Traveling for a month is way different than going on a simple 1 or 2-week vacation. You'll learn a tremendous amount about yourself.

In the following sections, we'll explore some realistic earning expectations, alternative career paths, as well as the location and lifestyle component of becoming a digital nomad. This will help to flesh out how the path will look for you going forward. That way, you can make more informed decisions, and when you're ready, take the leap.

CHAPTER 3:

The Average Digital Nomad Salary

How much money do digital nomads make?

Last year, I made $107k from my work as a blogger/ podcaster/ YouTuber. This comes from a variety of income sources. The first year that I went full-time, I made $30k, living in New York City as a location-independent entrepreneur. I was 22 years old.

It was *so freakin' scary* to be living in a major city and having to depend on the internet as my sole source of income. I was living on egg + cheese sammiches, ramen, and McDonalds.

I remember for my 22nd birthday, my girlfriend at the time bought me a cake. This was right around when the first season of House of Cards came out. Every night, I'd take an hour break from work. I'd lay down on my bed in my tiny $800 apartment in upper Harlem (which I shared with 4 other roommates), and watch House of Cards. I'd eat cake, drink milk, and try to resist the urge to binge watch the entire season.

Believe it or not, I made that cake last a week. Haha. It was literally my dinner for that entire week. Even though that initial year was very hard, I knew it would get better. Time and statistics were on my side.

If you're thinking of becoming a digital nomad, then getting an accurate answer as to how much you can expect to earn is extremely valuable. That's because, it will help you determine if you should alter your future and your career path.

You've heard about these people who earn money from their laptop, travel, take lots of Instagram pics (or vlogs) and manage to make it all work. You're wondering, is this lifestyle actually realistic?

I'm going to first cover why the actual answer varies so much, and then drill down into the hard numbers, statistics, and facts so that you can make the best decision possible.

Here's Why The Answer Varies So Much

The main reason why can be summed up pretty easily... not every digital nomad works full-time.

"Digital nomads are a mix of full-timers (54 percent) and part-timers (46 percent) and many only do it for part of a year." – MBO Partners.

If someone is not working full-time, then it's hard to judge their earned income against a person who's spending 40 hours per week in an office, staring at a computer screen. In addition, certain types of jobs are paid more than others. The average programmer is gonna make more than the average virtual assistant.

It would be a mistake to compare the average digital nomad salary for a programmer with that of a virtual assistant. It's an apples to orange comparison.

Rather than looking at the "average salary of a digital nomad," I would recommend looking at the average salary for someone who has the type of career you'd like to pursue. If you plan to use your writing skills to do freelance writing, blogging, and/or consulting while you are traveling, then look up the average salary for these types of jobs.

Are we on the same page? Good!

Lastly, some digital nomads are business owners. They may pay themselves a big or small salary depending on how they want to allocate their capital. Maybe they could afford to pay themselves $100k, but instead decide to pay themselves $50k and invest $50k back into the business in terms of ads, freelancers, and tools to make them more efficient at their job.

This investment might initially be considered an expense, but it could lead to future growth, which means even more income down the road. I know some business owners who don't even take a salary, because they're so focused on plowing all profits back into the business to grow it as quickly as possible.

Now, you can see why this question is difficult to answer. However, there *is* an answer for those of you who love data and straight numbers.

18% of Nomads report making six figures or more

This statistic is put out by Flexjobs. From my travels, my experience is that most of these nomads are either programmers or business owners.

A good programmer can easily make $100 – $150k per year. Their work is highly valued. Many programmers don't even have to work most of the year to make ends meet. It's very lucrative if you're good and you know what you're doing.

Along with earning income from freelancing, many of these programmers have side projects where they do things like build apps and sell them, make WordPress plugins for sale, or try starting a tech startup.

For business owners, the sky is the limit. It all depends on how effective you are at selling your products and your services. Likely, if you're getting into the upper numbers, you also have a team around you.

The one downside of being a business owner is that, if you're anything like me, you probably are almost addicted to working. A lot of these mega earners are pulling 60 to 80-hour work weeks.

This cuts into their ability to do fun things on a regular basis. It can also limit their ability to form certain types of relationships and connections while abroad. On the flip side, there is a huge upside to earn freedom, money, and the ability to be your own boss.

22% make between $50,000 and $99,999.

This is also a statistics put out by Flexjobs. I think it's a much more realistic number for the average person out there who's doing things like consulting, coaching, freelancing, and maybe some light online business work.

It's very easy to hit these numbers if you start freelancing and you command a healthy rate. However, it also takes up your time. You have to find a work-life balance in order to be happy as a digital nomad.

This is usually why I recommend diversifying your income sources so that you can earn a bit from freelancing, a bit from blogging, some from digital products, and other income from affiliate marketing.

Otherwise, you might risk pulling your hair out managing so many clients and having to always be online. You won't have any time to actually enjoy your time abroad.

Personally, I've found that the amount of money that I make doesn't really bring me more happiness.

What brings me happiness is the amount of money I can **SAVE**.

What brings me happiness is the difference between my income and expenses.

That money that goes into my savings is growing my wealth over time. I can use it to invest in stocks, real estate in the future, or to start new companies.

38 percent report earning less than $10,000 per year.

This statistic was put out by MBO Partners and speaks to a reality that I've also seen in my travels. A lot of digital nomads aren't making that much money.

But, it doesn't seem to bother them. That's because they are living in a country with a low standard of living. They don't have to pay very much to get by. In NYC, they'd be on the poverty line, but in Chiang Mai Thailand, they're doing fine.

There are tons of places around the world with a low standard of living that are perfect for digital nomads.

You also see a lot of these digital nomads who are just beginning to get their footing when it comes to things like online business, selling their services online, and figuring out how to market themselves.

Don't get discouraged. I've been there too. That's why I'm dedicated to helping you every step of the way, until you achieve location independence and are earning decent income at the same time.

If you dig deeper into the MBO Partners statistics, you'll also see that there are many nomads who only travel for part of the year. When they do travel, they aren't as concerned about making income.

They are earning some income from their freelancing work or location-independent business and drawing on their savings for any other expense they may need to cover.

"Others are nomadic for shorter periods, taking "workcations" and working sabbaticals lasting from several weeks to many months."- MBO Partners.

I like the idea of a sabbatical, because it lets me focus on new business projects and creative ideas. I used my most recent sabbatical to write a book in the spiritual niche called Unlocking Human Potential.

~22 percent make between $10k – $50k

Based on the other statistics out there, you can make this approximation. I also would say that around $30k is a very realistic number for the average person to earn during their digital nomad journeys.

This might be less than your current job, but the standard of living will also be very different abroad. At the end of the day, it's all up to you and how much time you want to spend working.

It's entirely possible for you to earn more, as the other statistics show above. You just have to make sure you're following a proven plan that works!

When I was getting started, I used to think that money was everything.

I wanted to be a very successful business owner (and I still do). But, my priorities have also changed.

I care more about living life than I do about padding my bank account.

When you're an old man or woman, do you want to be in your hospital bed, ruminating about all of the dreams you never tried?

Do you want to feel regret about that person you didn't ask out, or that job you didn't take?

NO!

<u>Life is too short to live with regret.</u>

Take a chance, try out the lifestyle, and in a couple of months you'll figure out whether or not it's for you.

You might end up wasting a little money, but I guarantee you'll discover a part of yourself that's more authentic than you've ever known. Get to know people around the world.

And – if you need a guide – keep reading!

You don't have to become some techie in order to make a living as a digital nomad. There are plenty of non-technical jobs out there that cater to individuals with a variety of skills. That's what we're going to get into next, so that you have the best chance of hitting the ground running quickly with this lifestyle.

CHAPTER 4:

Non-Technical Jobs for a Digital Nomad

So you want to become a digital nomad, but you ain't got no technical skills?

I hear ya loud and clear. So many location independent workers talk about programming as an easy way to break into the digital nomad scene, but what if you don't program?

Thankfully, there are lots of non-technical jobs out there aspiring digital nomads. I, myself, have a non-technical job.

I wanted to take some time to document the best ones with the highest earning potential and that are pretty easy to perform anywhere. You literally only need your laptop to get started in these career paths.

Online Writer

When I was in 9th grade English class, my teacher told me that writers don't make any money. Oh boy, was she wrong. I've had teachers and family members tell me my entire life that writers don't make good money, but they have all been proven to be incorrect.

In fact, I'd go so far as to say that becoming an online writer is one of the most lucrative career choices out there in the non-technical category. I built my *entire* online business off of writing.

There are different forms of writing which you should be aware of:

- **Blog post writing ($25 to $150 range for one article):** Informative or entertaining articles, blog pots, news, and online content.

- **SEO-optimized writing ($100-$125 for 600-750 word):** blog posts that are designed to attract traffic from search engines. Typically, 1k – 2k words, but not always.

- **Long-form content writing ($0.10-$0.20 per word):** ebooks, white papers, guides, and ghostwriter published work.

- **Copywriting ($80 – $120/hr):** marketing emails, sales pages, opt-in pages.

- **Technical writing ($0.25 per word):** explanation and material related to technical products.

- **Marketing writing ($50 – $100/hr):** press releases, social media, package inserts, etc.

- **MISC writing ($50 – $150/hr)):** grant writing, resumes, quizzes, legal.

I haven't even touched the service of editing, but obviously each of these verticals also include editing. The reason why I listed out all the form of writing is that the actual words and strategy that you use is **different**.

For example, a news article might be 500 words, but a SEO optimized blog post might be 2,500. A blog post might be wordy with lots of links and explanation, but a sales page has very few links, a distinct format, and the use of evocative emotional imagery. One is teaching and one is selling.

If you're looking to follow in my footsteps to become a six-figure writer, then I'd recommend getting started learning how to write blog posts and SEO-optimized blog posts. You can learn how to do that by reading my other book, Blogging for Beginners: Work from Home, Travel the World, Provide for Your Family by Salvador Briggman.

Then, I would begin to learn about copywriting, as copywriters can command a much higher rate than other forms of writers.

<u>**Online Marketing**</u>

Every business needs free social media traffic, and you can be there to deliver it to them. There are a lot of things that fall under the umbrella of online marketing, and lots of skills.

For example, you could become valuable from a design perspective, making people's FB page look pretty, or you could use effective tools to automate all of their social media and manage social media comments.

I'll list down below some opportunities that I see in this industry

- **Social media management ($500 – $1,000 per client per month):** You may have a few clients. You can manage their Facebook, FB Group, Instagram, LinkedIn, and others app that their customers are on. You'd be in charge of updates, content, and engagement.

- **Paid FB/Google Ads (percentage of spend):** You would be in charge of using paid Facebook or Google ads to deliver traffic to a client's website, generate leads, or build up their Facebook fan page.

- **PR and Media Outreach ($60 – $120/hr):** You gotta know what you're doing, but if you're able to get media hits for companies and individuals, this can be a valuable asset for many new product launches.

- **Video creation and design ($1 – 3k for video, 5-8k upper tier):** You can make or edit videos for a client's social media, ad campaigns, or YouTube channel. This may take knowing how to use an editor.

As you can see, there are lots of potential career paths. It comes down to your core skill set, and if you want to work in organic or paid marketing, as they are very different.

<u>**Virtual Assistant**</u>

You can become a virtual assistant and work for a CEO or a company doing various tasks that they need. There are a lot of functions that fall under the category of a virtual assistant. Also, different companies have different needs.

Typically, I'd group these needs together in a few different categories:

- Data entry

- Email outreach and coordination

- Scheduling

- Customer service

- Organizing internal company documents

- Logistics (flights/travel)

- Community management

- Database building

A lot of smaller companies, like mine, will use Virtual Assistants in a few different areas. They typically work for a few different companies.

<u>**Design & Illustration**</u>

While designers might not have been able to travel in the past, now a days, with powerful graphic design tools and the persistent need for good design, it's become a very lucrative career. All you need is your laptop and an internet connection.

Here are a few different types of design and illustration jobs:

- **Website design (non-technical):** I mean the layout, look and feel, color scheme, etc.

- **App design:** The user interface, colors, and overall look.

- **Social media:** Designing things like YouTube headers, Facebook covers, Infographics, etc.

- **Product Launches:** Designing product mockups, the look and feel of sales pages, logos.

- **Product Design:** Working on physical products and how they hold in the hand.

- **Comics, Animations:** Creating characters and illustrations to be used in animations or visual storytelling.

As you can see, it really depends on how you want to use your skills. Typically, if your work is tied to a large project, like a new up and coming product, you'll earn more money.

Online Business Owner

This is the route that I chose to go. Really, it's combining a few of your talents together to offer services, but also to create products, like books or courses, in order to make your keep.

You can also do things like affiliate marketing or making money from ads and sponsorships. Usually, it would be best to pick one core skillset and work outwards from there. For example, if you're a good designer, why not make a WordPress theme and then sell it on a marketplace like Themeforest.

These are a few simple online business owner expert ideas:

- **YouTuber:** Create YouTube videos, sell merchandise or your own products, make money from ads and sponsorships.

- **Blogger:** Earn your keep from freelance writing, affiliate marketing, ads, and digital products

- **Podcaster:** Make money from sponsorships, membership sites, coaching, and more.

- **Instagrammer:** Get attention through your photos and sell promoted posts, affiliate marketing, and your own services.

The reason why I like the business owner choice is that it gives you a tremendous amount of freedom compared to the other options.

Coach or Consultant

This is a very popular service now a days. As a consultant, you're using your existing knowledge to help companies solve problems. I do this occasionally with my own business.

The role of a coach is to help someone step by step through a process, where they're trying to achieve an end result. You help hold them accountable, but you also give them the tools to get there faster. The great thing about being a coach or a consultant is that you can easily do phone calls with your clients through Google voice or Skype, even if you're in a different country.

What's more, you can typically bundle other services as a coach, and upsell your services with things like online courses or books, which fit nicely into coaching packages.

These are the most popular industries for coaches:

- Life Coaching

- Dating and Relationships

- Business, Sales, Marketing.

- Spirituality

- Health and Wellbeing

- Career Achievement

You can find a lot of great niches out there to choose from!

Talent Jobs

When I say talent jobs, I'm referring to things like voice acting or video presenting. These usually are based off of an inborn talent that you have, be that modeling or speaking a certain way.

Talent jobs are a bit more difficult than some of the others out there, because the gigs and come and go. Your success will depend on your ability to maintain long-lasting clients and rapidly find new ones.

Here are few examples of talent gigs:

- Voice acting or voice over
- Video presenting or spokesperson
- Modeling
- Photography as you travel
- Video taking for businesses as you travel
- Teaching language
- Performing, selling jewelry, etc.

Throughout my travels, I have met people who do these types of things to earn their money as a digital nomad, but they usually aren't making very much. It's more of a "gig" model. I wouldn't depend on this one for a good income.

Now that you know about some of the available careers for non-technical people, I want to begin to explore the option of freelancing, because that's the fastest way to earn money. If you already have a job and you wanna quit it to go out on your own, freelancing is also the easiest transition. You'll just go from having one employer to a few clients. That's what we'll be focused on in the next chapter, and more importantly, how to be successful at it!

CHAPTER 5:

How to Become a Digital Nomad Freelancer

Freelancing is one of the fastest ways to generate income online.

Anytime you're selling a service, it's easier for a buyer to make sense of what you're offering.

This is why there are even specific websites out there dedicated to connecting business owners who need help with talented freelancers! In the last chapter, I went over a few different types of jobs that you can have as a digital nomad. Now, I want to cover a step-by-step plan for actually becoming a freelancer.

I'll walk you through what you'll need to do every step of the way, along with key resources and websites that will speed up the entire process. If you play your cards right, you can get set up in a matter of a week! Likely though, it will probably take you two or three to really get the ball rolling.

Let's dive into it, so that you can one day spend your time chilling on the beach, enjoying a beautiful dinner in a city with ancient architecture, or discover a new country that you might like to call home.

How Freelancers (*Actually*) Earn Money Online

I know it might sound straightforward, but freelancers actually earn money a little differently than you may have at your previous job. With your previous employer, all you had to do was convince one company to hire you. It happened one time. You showed up at their office with your resume for an interview. If you did well, you moved on through the interview process, and in a couple of weeks, you were hired. You were then guaranteed a source of recurring monthly revenue, your paycheck. As long as you showed up for work every day, and made sure to do a good job, you got that paycheck.

When it comes to freelancing, you are moving from job to job and client to client. Rather than having one boss, you will likely have multiple. Sometimes, that client will be paying you to work on a project over the course of a year. Other times, it might only be for a month. This is an important distinction, because it means that you need to create a strong user profile (or work portfolio) that you can easily and quickly send new clients should they ever ask. We'll get into that a little bit later. It also means that your income will vary from month to month. You are not guaranteed a salary.

As a beginning freelancer, you will likely be taking on lots of jobs to earn reviews and testimonials from your clients. This period is temporary for most types of jobs. Soon, you'll progress into having a few steady clients. To get through this initiation stage as quickly as possible, you'll want to zero in on the strategy that you'll use for your freelancing career.

Pick Your Profit, Passion, and Your Purpose

"Do not ignore your gift. Your gift is the thing **you do the absolute BEST with the LEAST amount of effort**." – Steve Harvey

Your profit will come from your skill. Your skill is the service that you'll be selling as a freelancer. This might be writing, marketing, coding, design, illustration, etc. There are so many of them out there. It's how you're gonna be raking in that *profit*, which makes up the Profit, Passion, and Purpose equation. Profit + Passion + Purpose = Freelancing Success.

Your skill determines your profitability as a freelancer

Put simply, the skill that you choose will determine your earning potential. I advise you to pick something that you're already good at, or that you'd like to become better at. If your skill relates to your current job, then it will be faster and easier to begin to earn money online. However, it's not a requirement.

You might hate your existing job. You might despise what you have to do to earn for a living. Sound familiar? Well, this an opportunity to begin an entirely new career. It's a chance to explore some of the hidden talents that you might have.

Here are some common digital nomad freelancing skills:

- Writing
- IT/Coding/Programming
- Marketing
- Designers
- Content creators
- Virtual assistant

Your skill doesn't have to fall into one of these categories. Remember, there are many. However, you should have an idea of the value that you're bringing to a potential client. Similar to a traditional job interview, they are going to assess how skilled you are and how you can fit into their organization.

Specialize your skills around your passions

As a freelancer, your core skill differs from your passion. Your passion relates more closely to the specific application of your skill. For example, my main skill when I was starting out was writing. However, my passion was educating about crowdfunding. So, the way I used my skill was to **write** lots and lots of blog posts and books about crowdfunding, which started my online career.

While writing might be your *core skill*, it can be used in many different ways. You could specialize in writing blog posts, ghostwriting ebooks, putting together marketing emails, or even writing sales pages using copywriting tactics. Think of your passion as your unique specialization within the overall skill. For me, that passion is using my skills to teach about particular subjects. I do that through blog posts, books, training courses, and coaching programs.

Writing is my core skill, but I've specialized it around my passions. Believe it or not, but I'm a horrible writer when it comes to writing fiction stories. A few years ago, when I went back to El Salvador in search of my birth mother, I wrote a memoir called Little Thumb of America. It details my search, along with some of my painful coming of age experiences as a Latino growing up in a white community. It's available on Amazon. It took me 6 months to write it. The writing process took so much time and dedication, that I questioned whether or not I'd ever get to the end. This adoption story was true, but I had to do a lot more visual storytelling and narration than I was used to. It was a slow, laborious writing experience. While I can quickly write a nonfiction book, fiction is a whole other story.

At this stage in my life, I use my writing as a vehicle for teaching. Someday, I may sit down and dedicate a year to working on a fiction novel, but it's not my passion right now. Writing is my skillset and teaching is my passion. Teaching is the specific application of how I use my writing to serve humanity. Does that make sense?

To begin to think about how you'd like to specialize (and thus infuse your work with passion), you should first consider the format in which you'd like to use your skill. Do you want to create financial websites for clients or set up ecommerce stores? Do you want to create mobile apps for clients or set up/maintain Wordpress websites? Begin to think about how you'd specifically like to use your gift.

You find purpose through your impact on the world

You might be coming to realize that your specialty is based on how you'd like to **help other people.** As I mentioned, I enjoy teaching, so I like seeing people learn things, apply them, and get results. I like breaking down complicated processes into easy-to-follow systems.

While your specialty is how you apply your skill, your purpose is derived from the vision that you have to impact the world. It's how you fit into the big picture. This is critically important for your freelancing journey because it is the source of your motivation. On the difficult days, you can always remember your purpose, and get a boost of vitality to continue on through difficulties.

Think about it... your previous employer has a mission. Right?

Their company has values. They have things they believe in. **Why is that?**

It's because when there is a mission, or a desired impact the company wants to make, it's much easier to motivate employees. When there is a common vision, the troops will assemble. They'll fight day and night to make that vision a reality.

Since you are now self-employed, you need your own form of this vision. It comes down to how you wanna help the world using your skill and your specialty. Profit + Passion + Purpose = Freelancing Success.

Showcasing Your Credibility – Creating Your Work Portfolio

Let's be honest. Degrees don't really matter.

There! I said it!

Yes, of course, some employers will look at where you went to school. But, more often than not, they're more interested in what you can tangibly do for them. So, they'll look at your work history. They'll ask you about the projects you've completed.

As a freelancer, your credibility comes in three forms:

- Your work history. What you've done for others. Your work portfolio.

- Your testimonials and reviews. How much money you've earned on a freelancing website.

- What you specifically say that you can do for an employer. This may be communicated with a cover letter or replying to a post. You're promising some kind of result.

Your Work History

This goes without saying, but you should definitely put any relevant projects or jobs you've done on your freelancing profile. I'll talk a bit about this profile and major freelancing marketplaces a bit later on.

In addition, you should also have a section of your personal website that details some of the work you've done in the past, for which clients, and the results that you've gotten them. The more that you can visually show potential clients your work, the faster they will start believing your claims. Without visual proof, clients have to take your word for it. Your credibility won't be as high as another freelancer who can show proof of their work.

Lastly, I would recommend putting together a folder that you can easily email clients should they ask for more details. This will vary from industry to industry, but they may want a sample of your work to see how good you are. Don't skimp on the look and feel of whatever you send over. If you're using something like PowerPoint or Keynote to demonstrate the projects you've worked on, make sure it looks pretty. I'd even spend a couple of bucks to have a designer make it look nice and professional.

Collect Testimonials and Reviews

Basically, these two items will form the "social proof" signals that a potential employer will be looking for when they stumble on your email or message. They want to know that they are making a good decision, so they'll look at certain trust factors.

If you're on a major freelancing marketplace, then they'll be sure to examine the various reviews you've gotten on that platform. They may look at the specific reviews, or the aggregate rating that you've received.

For potential clients that you're reaching out to, or that stumble on your website, they'll want some assurances that if they decide to hire you and sign a contract, that you won't quickly turn into a mistake. One of the easiest ways to begin to get testimonials is to go on LinkedIn and start asking your previous bosses to leave a LinkedIn recommendation. Formally, you could also send previous bosses an email or a letter asking for a testimonial. Make sure you explain the reason.

The more testimonials and reviews that you have, the easier it is for a potential employer to say that it's a "no-brainer" decision to hire you.

Tailor Your Employer Communications

This isn't done by a lot of freelancers.

Most freelancers will usually send some kind of boilerplate message to potential employers that's not at all customized for the job.

When you respond to a job posting, or email a prospective client, this is a marketing opportunity for you to stand out above other freelancers! Show them that you know what they're looking for. Demonstrate how you've completed similar jobs in the past, and what you can *DO* for them if they hire you.

When someone replies to one of my job posting with a custom message along with some ideas related to the job posting, it shows me they are already thinking critically and will be a go-getter if I hire them for the job.

Rather than relying on an employer to go through the work of looking through your work history or portfolio, you can draw their attention to a few bullet items, and specifically, **how** you can help them with the specific project.

It also shows that you care, which is always a positive trait.

Pricing Yourself

Pricing yourself correctly as a freelancer can make the difference between barely scraping by and being able to live the lifestyle of your dreams. If you're thinking of just taking your salary and dividing that number by the number of hours in a year... think again!

Let's just say that you earn $50,000 per year. There are 52 weeks in a year, and you work 40 hours per week, so you assume that there are 2,080 hours you work per year.

You divide $50,000 by 2,080 and get... $24 per hour. So that should be your hourly wage, right?

WRONG!

Let me explain why. As an employee of a company, there are certain luxuries that you are afforded which we call employee benefits. These include:

- Paid sick days, vacation days, national holidays

- Health insurance. Dental/vision insurance.

- Retirement benefits

- Workplace perks (laptop, cell phone, WIFI, office space, coffee etc.)

- There are many others, but the ones above are the main ones.

When you're a freelancer, you don't get any of these, so you have to calculate them into your hourly rate if you want to be able to do things like take sick days or take vacation days.

Step 1: Subtract Freelancing Costs From Your Salary ($50,000)

What are some of the common costs that come with being a freelancer?

Some include:

- Shared office space
- Website hosting
- Accounting/invoicing software
- Marketing tools
- New laptop
- Tax and accounting fees
- Other types of software
- Healthcare
- Self-employment tax

Let's assume that this all comes out to be about $12,000 per year.

$50,000 + $12,000 = $62,000

Step 2: Figure Out How Much Time Is Billable

This is a fancy way of saying, figure out how much time you spend actually doin' work. Assuming you work 40 hours per week, 52 weeks a year. That's 2,080 work hours.

If you take a standard 3-week vacation, which is fifteen 8-hour days, that's 120 hours you gotta knock off your billable time. If you take 7 US holidays, then that will be 7×8 or 56 hours you gotta knock off as well. Finally, if you take 5 sick days, that's 5×8 = 40 hours you gotta knock off too.

So…. 2,080 – 120 – 56 – 40 = 1,864 billable hours per year you'll be workin'.

Step 3: Figure Out How Much You'll ACTUALLY Be Working

I don't know about you, but I don't spend every waking hour serving a client.

Some of my time is spent marketing myself, getting new clients, doing emails, social media, etc.

Let's assume that when you're staring out, you're spending 50% of your time "working on the business" and 50% of your time actually working for new clients. By working on the business, I'm referring to all those miscellaneous to-do items like accounting, legal items, setting up the website, building social media profiles, writing blog posts, and other items.

As you progress, that might be closer to a 25% on the business and 75% on clients split. But for now, let's just assume it's 50/50.

So… 1,864*.50 = 932 billable hours you'll *actually* be working per year.

Step 4: Divide Your Target Salary by Calculated Hours

Now, we'll go back to step 1 and take your calculated new salary, which is $62,000 and divide that by 932 hours.

We have concluded that to comfortably ease into the freelancing life, *you'd need to charge $66.52/hour.*

That might seem like a lot, but if you feel uncertain, you could go back into our little equation and change up some things.

For example, if you intend to work 75% of the time, and only spend 25% on business (or also work on weekends to get done miscellaneous tasks), this would allow you to decrease your target hourly rate substantially.

In this case, you'd *only have to make $44/hour* to make a decent living.

As another example, if you decided that you weren't going to take any vacation, sick days, or US holidays, then you could take those numbers out of the equation.

In this case, you'd *only have to make $39/hour* to make a decent living.

Step 5: Stick To Your Rate Strategy

You could decide to really hustle in your first year as a freelancer and not take off any sick days, holidays, or vacation days. You could also decide to work 7 days a week. These are all killer ways to make sure you charge an affordable rate, which means more clients.

However, after some period of time, you'll become burnt out. Eventually, you need to have some type of a normal life. By sticking to the model that I outlined above, you'll ensure that your freelancing rate takes into account the lifestyle that you want to lead.

If you want to stick to your guns, maintain a good lifestyle, and not have to worry about working yourself to the bone, then command the rate that you think makes sense. It might be a little scary to charge a high rate, but you'll thank me later. You're simply charging what is required to maintain your current standard of living.

Also, the good news is that when you're traveling overseas to other countries, the standard of living will be much lower. You won't have to earn the same amount that you did back home. This means your money will go much further than before.

<u>**Finding Work as a Freelancer**</u>

You've figured out your talent, passion, and your purpose. Now, it's time to hunt down those initial jobs and gigs that are gonna bring cash in the door.

There are many practical strategies for finding good work opportunities online. I like to break them down into these specific categories:

- **Freelancing websites:** These are marketplaces where companies go to hire freelancers. They will put out a job posting that you can reply to. Companies will also browse the site and hire freelancers based off of their profile information.

- **Your personal network:** The employers that you have had before may be willing to hire you on a freelancing basis. You also have many colleagues who may refer work to you. These are all the companies and connections you've touched in your professional life.

- **Your marketing efforts:** The active ways in which you are marketing your services to business owners you don't know. This might include social media, thought leadership, direct emails, and more.

Each of these strategies can work to get you jobs initially and in the long run. They all have various benefits and drawbacks. I'm going to go through each of them and nail down exactly how you can use each to find more work.

<u>**Freelancing Websites to Find Freelancing Jobs**</u>

Let's start with some of the websites out there that you can browse to find freelancing work. Each of these sites are very different depending on their fees, types of freelancers, and how the platform works. I'd take a little bit of time to look into each of them.

1. Upwork

Upwork is my favorite website out of this list. I hire a lot of my own freelancers off of them. The first step is to create an account on Upwork. It might seem straightforward, but remember, your account is basically like your resume.

It's easy for you to find work, connect with employers, get paid, and everything happens through the website, so that you don't have to deal directly with companies regarding invoices.

It's very straightforward. The only downside is that you may deal with lots of competition from places like India, so make sure you have a good profile and tailored cover letter.

Pricing: "Upwork charges contractors a 20%, 10%, or 5% service fee depending on the total amount they've billed with a client." On the employer's side, there is a 3% processing fee on payments.

2. Freelancer

Freelancer is another main freelancing website that you can use to find jobs. You can list any career-related skills under the sun and get paid for your time. It's easy to manage everything from their website.

As a member on Freelancer, you can create an account for free and you get up to 8 job bids per month. After that, you can decide to increase the job bids you have available to you.

Personally, I don't use Freelancer to hire freelancers because their fee structure is kind of confusing, charges companies, and I haven't seen as good quality as other sites.

Pricing: "The fee for fixed price projects is 10% or $5.00 USD, whichever is greater, and 10% for hourly projects." "If you are subsequently hired to perform that Service, a 20% fee of the total service price is charged."

3. Guru

Guru is a great site to find work under a variety of categories like writing & editing, design, programming, etc. It's very easy to set up a profile, browse the marketplace, and apply to jobs.

This site isn't as well-known as some of the others, but it is a valuable weapon in your arsenal. You can also very easily browse jobs even if you don't have a user account.

Guru charges fees to both employers and employees. For employers, it's a 2.9% handling fee on the invoice value of your freelancer.

Pricing: "We charge a small job fee on the invoice value to the Freelancers. The job fee ranges from 5% to 9% depending on their membership level." Employers can choose to cover this fee, split it, or have the freelancer bear it.

4. Toptal

This is a bit of a different kind of freelancing website. They make you go through an application process and make a $500 deposit to weed out people who aren't serious.

They bill themselves as the place to find top talent, and thus will charge higher rates than other marketplaces in the industry. There is a bit more hand holding on the part of employers than other sites.

They charge a fixed hourly rate to employers depending on the job and no recruiting fee. I wish they would be a bit more transparent with how they earn money, but it seems like it's the difference between what they charge employers and what they pay freelancers. That could be 50/50. The site doesn't say unfortunately.

"Nontransparent fees/rates. They usually take 70% of what clients pay for your work. Banning from network when a developer becomes "inconvenient". If you ask for a raise, they might ban you from the network. That's how "you set your own rate"". – Glassdoor.

<u>**5. Fiverr**</u>

As an employer, Fiverr is my other favorite website aside from Upwork. As a Freelancer, it's a very easy way to get started earning income online by selling your services. There is also now a new initiative, Fiverr Pro, which is for higher-end services.

It's free to join the website and you can list many different types of services from the comfort of your home. You can also offer different versions of your service and charge from $5 – $995 (or more with Pro).

When you're paid, the money is transferred immediately into your account, so it makes for less waiting time.

Pricing: "There is no subscription required or fees to list your services. You keep 80% of each transaction."

<u>Get Freelancing Gigs From Your Personal Network</u>

Your own network is also a great source for freelancing jobs!

Remember, these are people who know you in some kind of professional capacity. These people have:

- Seen your work.
- They have a sense of your character.
- You've worked for them before.

<u>Your Old Bosses</u>

You can first start with your old bosses. As long as you've maintained a good relationship, they won't have any issue with you emailing them to do a discovery call and see if you can add value to any of the projects at the company.

Talented and motivated workers are hard to find. Most companies will scoop them up when they can. If you demonstrate that you can add value to any ongoing projects, then this might be a quick win for you.

The only difficulty with this approach is that after the project is complete, you'll have to continue to find ways to add value to the company. Most companies that pay staff regularly do so because they have their exclusive and undivided attention. As a freelancer, you're a hired gun, so you will be working for many companies, not just them.

Your Colleagues

In addition, you can ping your colleagues to see what the environment is at their company when it comes to hiring. Sometimes, new verticals are expanding rapidly, and companies are hungry on the lookout for talent. Other times, a company isn't doing any hiring. By finding this information out first, you can decide whether or not you should even float the idea of working in a freelance capacity.

This might be a little anxiety producing at first, but remember, this is why you formed the connections in the first place! So that you can help them out, and they can help you out. Otherwise, what's the point? Unless you're friends in the course of your normal life, your colleagues are there to strengthen your career.

I would recommend taking a personal approach through phone and in-person meetings because often times, it's hard to really get a full picture of how a "lead" is feeling from just email. They might tell you that there are many opportunities, but they are just saying that to be nice. You need to be able to judge from their body language and tone of voice.

Your Industry Connections

Lastly, your industry connections are an amazing source of leads when it comes to finding freelancing opportunities. These are different from your colleagues. They are comprised of:

- Clients of your previous employer

- Competitors to your previous employer

- Similar companies in the industry

You can tap into your industry connections, who may have also seen your performance at your previous job. If not, they will likely be aware of your skill set and what you can bring to the table. It's a lot easier to get someone who already knows you and your value to consider you for a freelancing opportunity.

Find Freelancing Opportunities From Your Marketing Efforts

You can also find freelancing jobs by marketing your skills. There are many ways to go about doing this. You might not be used to marketing yourself, but it's very common in the freelancing world.

When it comes to getting the word out about your skills, there are several key strategies:

- **Thought leadership:** Writing articles on LinkedIn or other major publications sharing your advice or expert opinion on key topics

- **Content marketing:** Putting out blog articles, YouTube videos, or podcast episodes that are helpful and informational. They are aimed at your target market.

- **Social media marketing:** Growing business-focused social media accounts on Twitter, Facebook, or Instagram to promote your content, thought leadership pieces, or your overall brand.

- **PR and public relations:** Reaching out to podcasts and media publications to share your expertise on key issues. This can be a great way to improve your credibility, while also getting more clients.

I would recommend getting started with thought leadership. You can easily write articles on LinkedIn or medium to begin to share your expertise with the world.

You should also set up a website that can house your work. Wix has a really easy tool that allows you to do this. There are lots of beautiful templates to choose from, and they are all easy drag and drop sites.

One of the things that I like about Wix is that it's very affordable, easy to use, and doesn't require any coding knowledge.

Marketing Yourself as a Freelancer

In order to get better quality jobs, you have to be willing to market your freelancing services.

When it comes to your services, the first way that you'll begin to market your services is by setting up an effective profile that clearly conveys what value you bring to business owners and clients.

Crafting the Perfect Profile

Your freelancing profile should not only show what you can do for others, but also underscore your trustworthiness, credibility, and provide a work history that will make you an enticing job candidate.

First of all, you're going to want to narrow in on what services you are offering. What is your expertise? How can you help others? This should be crystal clear. Think about what a potential employer would want to read if they were hiring for a job.

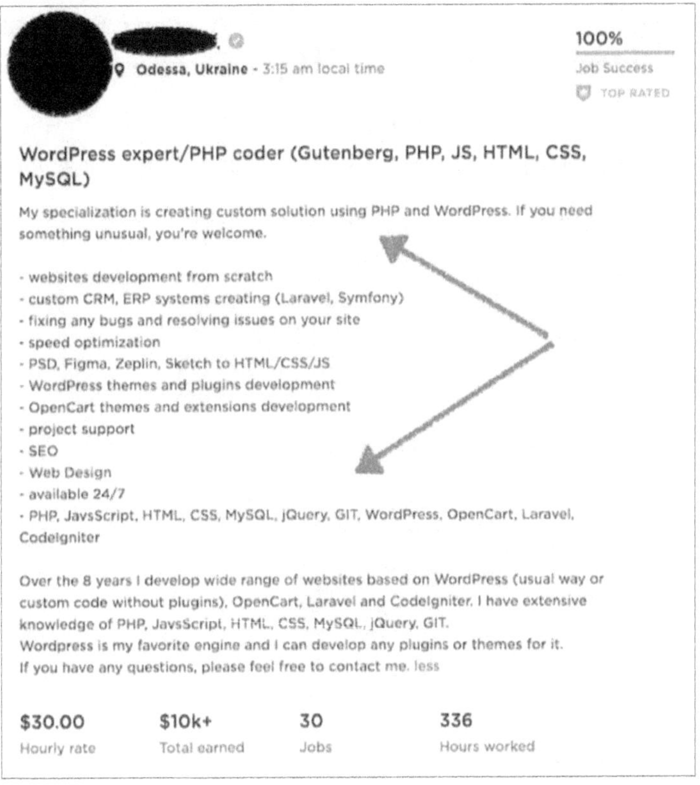

All too often, I will come across freelancing profiles that are vague, or that focus on too many different skill sets. Unless you're providing something like virtual assistant services, you don't want to be a generalist. You want to be a specialist.

Most companies are pretty smart. If you list too many different skills, they may see you as a jack of all trades, but a master of none. You can't be good at everything. I don't want a to hire a programmer to maintain my website who also is focused on selling services as a writer, social media content creator, video editor, and audio producer. If they're going to be working on my website, I want them to be super good at that job.

Mastering the Cover Letter

After you've put some work into your freelancing profile, then you'll want to begin to think about the cover letter that you use to respond to various jobs that are listed on freelancing marketplaces.

This cover letter should be tailored for each job. You don't want to paste the same generic text for each one. This will make it virtually impossible to stand out from the crowd of other freelancers who are trying to get the job.

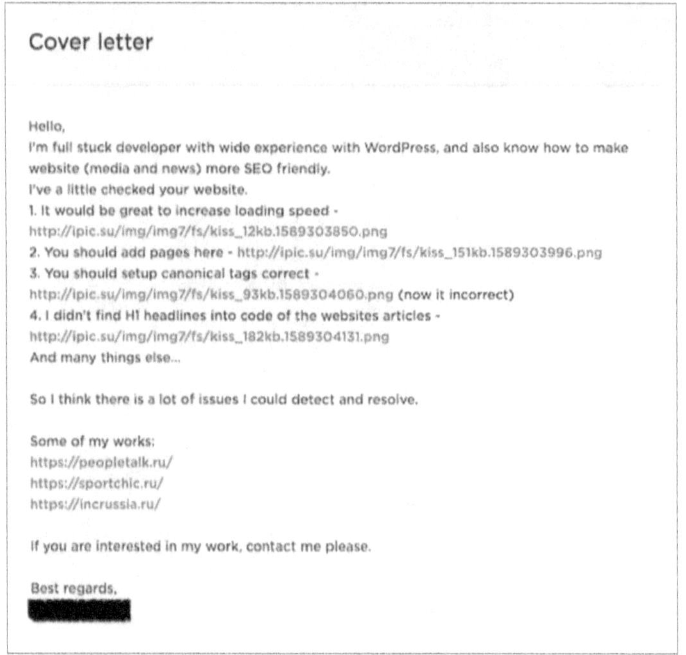

Cover letter

Hello,
I'm full stuck developer with wide experience with WordPress, and also know how to make website (media and news) more SEO friendly.
I've a little checked your website.
1. It would be great to increase loading speed -
http://ipic.su/img/img7/fs/kiss_12kb.1589303850.png
2. You should add pages here - http://ipic.su/img/img7/fs/kiss_151kb.1589303996.png
3. You should setup canonical tags correct -
http://ipic.su/img/img7/fs/kiss_93kb.1589304060.png (now it incorrect)
4. I didn't find H1 headlines into code of the websites articles -
http://ipic.su/img/img7/fs/kiss_182kb.1589304131.png
And many things else...

So I think there is a lot of issues I could detect and resolve.

Some of my works:
https://peopletalk.ru/
https://sportchic.ru/
https://incrussia.ru/

If you are interested in my work, contact me please.

Best regards,

One easy way to get someone's attention is to prove that you read their posting. You can:

- **Reiterate back what they are looking for.** Ex. "I see you're looking for ___. I have experience doing ___."

- **Diagnose their problem.** Ex. "I took a look at your ___. It seems like ___. I can help with this because ___."

- **Draw their attention to your portfolio.** Ex. "I was reading through ___ and I actually completed a very similar job called ______ if you look at my portfolio. It was a smash success. Would love to help you _____."

- **Inject emotion into your response.** Ex. "You have amazing ____. I'm passionate about ___ and I've _____. I'd love to help on this. Reply if you have any questions. I completed a recent job that's similar called ______."

Many times, employers are receiving so many cover letters that your first task should simply be to get their attention. By injecting emotion, diagnosing their problem, or proving that you read their posting, you're far more likely to get a reply than the cookie-cutter standard replies they typically get.

This will instantly snag their attention, because you seem like a real human being on the other side. You've taken the time to understand the job, which means that you will also be careful in understanding their instructions in the future. It shows thoughtfulness and critical thinking skills.

Setting up Your Marketing Engine

Your website is your home base.

It's where anyone can go to find out more information about you. It adds tremendous legitimacy to your freelancing practice.

If you don't plan to do any kind of "content marketing" where you write blog posts on your website and you only intend to use your website to house your portfolio and basic information, then I'd recommend setting up a Wix website.

It's very easy to get started. Everything is drag and drop. There are lots of beautiful templates that you can choose from. You'll have a professional-looking website for a fraction of the cost.

However, if you want to set up your own blog where you can share insights, thoughts, and educational content which will attract potential clients, then I gotta suggest that you look into Bluehost.

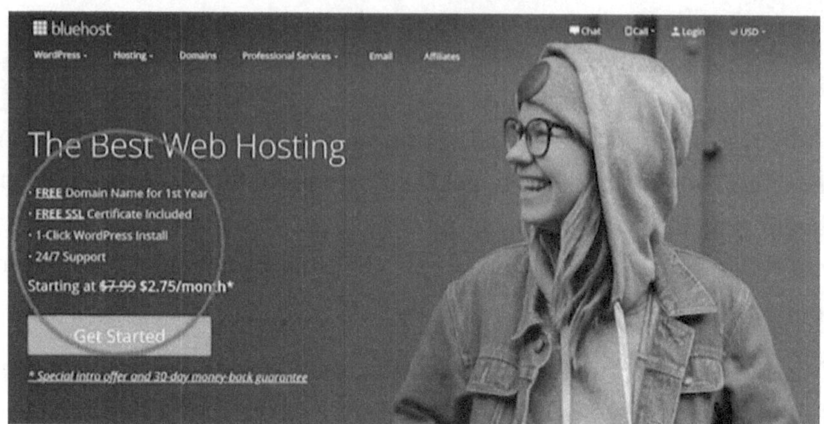

These guys are masters when it comes to helping you set up a blog using WordPress. You get a free domain name when you sign up, as well as a free SSL certificate (think security). Not to mention, they have 24/7 support. You can talk with real people!

WordPress is the backbone of most blogs. It's a powerful and robust framework (that I also use) to set up a blog. Using WordPress, you'll also be able to install useful plugins and other functionality to do things like accept online payments.

From this point on, anytime you share a bit of content that's housed on your blog, visitors will come to your website and learn about your freelancing services. How cool is that? It's free marketing! You just have to write blog articles, share them, and you'll get traffic. Then, people will be able to discover more about how you can help their business.

I find that this works really well in particular if you're offering things like freelance writing services. It's also great for promoting social media marketing services. Soon, you won't even have to write new blog articles. You can share the old ones on social media and keep getting recurring traffic to your blog. That traffic then translates into new clients for your business.

You'll have so many that you won't know what to do with them!

When you get to this point, you'll be able to raise your rates, since you have more demand than you can handle. You'll be making more money in less time.

Branching Out From Freelancing

Freelancing is a great way to start to earn some fast income online. After all, if you have a valuable skillset and can prove your worth, then it's very easy to make sense of hiring you for a project.

That being said, in the long run, the career can be a little bit constraining, and here's why.

As a freelancer, you're selling your time for money.

You're not building up an asset which can produce income.

You're using your main asset, which is time, to earn income.

If you fall sick, your income will dry up.

If you have to take care of a loved one and can't work, then you won't get paid.

If you max out your time with lots of clients, you hit your earning limit.

So, what can you do?

Thankfully, other freelancers have already answered that question!

Let's take an example. Let's say that you do freelance writing services.

Most of your time throughout the week is spent writing articles for your clients, but on the weekends, you work on you own projects. You do things like:

- **Start a blog:** Write articles, get traffic from search engines/social media, and make money from ads, affiliate marketing, and digital products.

- **Write an ebook:** Make passive income from Amazon, or sell the ebook independently on your own website.

- **Teach inside a membership community:** Maybe, once a week, you teach writing inside of a membership community where people pay to get access to your training.

- **Create an online course:** Another form of passive income, online courses are not only a great way to share your learnings, but also a way you can make money on autopilot.

- **Hire sub-contractors:** Have other lower-paid writers work for you in helping to produce content for clients. This way, you become more of a manager.

When you take ANY of these steps, you begin to transition from simply offering freelancing services to stepping into the role of a business owner.

Branching out as a freelancer does require you to learn new skills and take on more responsibility, but there is also tremendous upside. Now, if you were to fall ill, you will still be making passive income from your digital products, advertising, affiliate marketing, and other revenue streams.

Think of it as a failsafe, so that you don't always have to depend on working yourself to the bone just to make ends meet. You can step up, become a business owner, and embrace being a leader.

I was talking about this concept with one of my blogging students and relaying a story back from the early days of my career.

I was 23 years old and while I was determined to work hard to earn money, it just felt like there was never enough of it. Every day, I would boot up my laptop and get to work. My bank account was starting to go up, but for some reason, it didn't feel like I was making any real progress.

At the end of the year, I looked at my bank account. The interest income was measly, at best, and the income I was generating from my investments in the stock market were barely enough to cover my apartment's utilities.

I could spend years and years saving up $100,000, and still, based on a good 10% return, still only generate $10,000 per year in passive income from my portfolio.

YUCK! That wouldn't even be enough to cover my rent in New York City.

Then, I realized something. Based the income I was generating from affiliate marketing and advertising, I was poised to make more than $10,000 that year in passive income.

It didn't make sense to me.

I could spend 10 years saving $100,000…. which would earn $10,000 per year in passive income.

Or, I could spend 1-year writing articles on my blog… which would earn more than $10,000 in passive income from affiliate marketing, advertising, and digital product sales. These articles continue to get traffic, years later.

WHAT!?!?

Haha, it was like a lightbulb moment went off in my head.

Why was I focused on just squirreling away money? I should be focused on building more passive income streams!

And, that's exactly what I did.

I still continue to build passive income streams to this day.

As the years go by, the amount of time that I need to trade for money goes down, and my passive income streams go up.

I talk a ton about this in the Digital Nomad Blueprint Course. Basically, it's what allows many of the digital nomads that you might know to travel the world, without having to break their backs working every second of every day.

Instead, they can go to Bali and actually relax!

They can visit an ancient Cambodian temple, without feeling like they're losing money in the process.

Believe it or not, but you can actually save money while you travel. You just need to go about it the right way.

I won't lie to you though. This transition does take work. You must be hungry and be willing to become something greater. To get started as a freelancer, I recommend checking out some of the website and resources that I mentioned above. However, keep this idea in the back of your mind of becoming a business owner.

In my travels around the world, I've come across so many freelancers with different verticals, skill sets, and passions. There's no reason why you can't join the ranks. I'd go so far as to say that this is the best time to become a freelancer! You have everything at your disposal. Take action, get started today, and you'll thank me that you did.

If nothing else, you will learn a lot, grow a ton, and come to realize that you can earn money anywhere – all that you need is a laptop and of course, a good internet connection. Also, a nice cocktail or a strong cup of coffee doesn't hurt either ;). Before we get into the best communities around the world for digital nomads, I want to share with you a few easy ideas to start a business. If you're not interested in starting a business, you can skip the next chapter. If you are, then listen up! Some of these business ideas have the potential to be extremely lucrative in the coming years.

CHAPTER 6:

Killer Digital Nomad Business Ideas

Setting up an online business is one of the easiest ways to become a digital nomad. When you are your own boss, you get to decide when you want to work. You get to pick the projects you work on. For this reason, it can have tremendous appeal to lovers of freedom, who want to exercise control over their life. There are lots of simple ways to earn income online. It all comes down to your skills, resources, and passion.

The first time that I traveled to Thailand as a digital nomad, I was earning money from my blog and marketing services. I was stupid and didn't sublet my apartment back in New York (more on that later). However, if I had, I would have actually saved money while traveling. I felt extremely thankful to be able to have a steady stream of income while I was abroad. I had heard horror stories of other travelers who had drained their savings account and ran out of money midway through the trip. I'd also talked with other "nomads" who quit their day jobs, traveled the world, and ended up returning home with thousands of dollars of credit card debt. As you're traveling around the world, this business will help to fund your lifestyle. It will prevent you from making bad financial decisions.

It can be hard to come up with your own business idea that's a good fit for the digital nomad lifestyle, so I wanted to put together a few for you. I'll divide them up based on the obligations required to keep them going, and hopefully get your mind churning as to ways you can set up a location-independent income source.

Service-Based Businesses

A service-based business is one where you trade your time for money. You can also have subcontractors or employees work underneath you and trade *their time* for money.

<u>The pros of a service-based business include:</u>

- Easy to set up with minimal investment

- Faster to make income online

- Opportunity for growth over time

<u>The cons of a service-based business include:</u>

- Limited profitability in the long run

- Selling time, so not as scalable

- Requires regular management and communication

<u>Here are some easy digital nomad service business ideas:</u>

There are SO MANY business ideas out there. All you gotta do is pick one sophisticated tool, skillset, or service… and master it! You'll be surprised how many business ideas can spring out of this kind of framework.

Marketing Agency: You can start a new marketing agency that helps business owners or individuals get exposure for their products and services. This could include organic marketing, influencer marketer, content marketing, paid media buying, PR, and more.

Blog Post Writing and Editing: You can become a freelance writer and editor. This will give you the segue to start a writing and editing business, where you hire subcontractors do things like write articles, books, whitepapers, ebooks, and more.

Podcast Transcription and Show Notes: Many companies now a days are looking for help managing their podcast. They want to hire writers who can help them produce a quality show transcript, and show notes for the accompanying blog post.

Podcast Management Agency: You'll take care of all the scheduling of podcast guests, setting them up with the host, scheduling the shows to go out, and even promoting the episodes. You'll also help the show get iTunes reviews.

YouTube Video Editing: Why not offer YouTube editing services to major businesses that are looking to expand their web presence. You can help them put together educational videos or edit any that they have already. You an even help them manage their channels using TubeBuddy.

Instagram and Facebook Videos: Many companies are looking for specific videos for Instagram and Facebook. These could be simple commercials, educational content, or engaging videos. You can use tools like Typito or Animoto to do this.

Visual explanations and Infographics: By mastering a simple application like Videoscribe or an infographics tools like Piktochart, you can set these up for your clients.

Photo Editing and Illustration: Now a days, with blog posts, YouTube videos, Facebook pages, and more, there's in need of an affordable service that will handle all your graphic design needs. You can use simple apps like Canva to offer this.

Simple Website Design: I can't count the number of people who are clueless about simple apps like Shopify, SquareSpace, and even WordPress. If you know the ins and outs of these simple tools, you can brand yourself as an "ecommerce website expert" or an expert at helping people upgrade their blog, using marketplaces like Themeforest.

Virtual Assistant: This works best if you specialize in some kind of industry. For example, you can be a virtual assistant that helps writers research for their books. That would be an example of specializing.

Digital Product Businesses

I recommend that all aspiring digital nomads dabble in the digital product game. These types of businesses are freakin' powerful. They are very easy to scale, can create passive income, and make it so you don't rely on selling your time.

Pros of a digital product business:

- No cost to deliver product, very profitable

- Highly scalable when a good marketing avenue is found

- Can be a source of passive income

Cons of a digital product business:

- Typically requires an investment of either time or money

- Marketing knowledge is required

- Make take longer to begin to earn revenue

Here are some easy digital nomad digital product business ideas:

Most of these businesses would exist in a larger niche, like fitness, wealth generation, dating, cooking, etc. Just take any non-fiction book genre, and usually you'll find a vertical within that.

Develop Website Themes and Plugins: You need a bit of coding knowledge to be able to do this, or you gotta hire a programmer. You can develop WordPress themes and plugins and either sell them on your own website or through an online marketplace. I have a friend doing this on Shopify making thousands and thousands per month.

Books, ebooks, and audio books: If you have an expertise, then this is the way to go for sure. I've written seven books and they are a powerful source of passive income. If you love writing and know what you're talking about, they're also a great way to expand your brand.

Online courses and programs: Simply getting started on a website like Udemy or Skillshare is good. You could then graduate to selling courses through your own marketing and using sophisticated systems to charge high-ticket prices.

Membership websites and mastermind groups: These are ALL the rage in the internet marketing world. They're attractive because you can charge a subscription membership price to be a part of one of these, meaning you'll get dependable, recurring revenue.

Online Coaching Hybrid Programs: You can typically combine the above business ideas with some type of coaching business, where you either do group coaching or high-ticket one-on-one coaching. This is selling your time, so it's more of a hybrid model.

Selling Photos and Music: You can license photos that you've taken and sell them on websites where marketers like me go to buy great-looking pics. Shuttershock is a simple example of this for photos. There are many others.

Mobile Apps: Another way that you can start a digital product as a digital nomad is to launch a new mobile app that users pay to use, or that has in-app purchases. This may require an investment.

Physical Product Businesses

In my travels, I've also met a lot of digital nomad entrepreneurs who have physical-product ventures. This means that they are selling real physical products to customers. They have some kind of an online storefront, like Shopify, and sell it that way.

Pros of a physical product business

- Can feel "more real" and be rewarding

- More scalable than services

- Ability to build a team around business

<u>**Cons of a physical product business**</u>

- Requires upfront investment

- Relies on supply chain

- Hard to enforce patents or trademarks

<u>Here are some easy physical product digital nomad businesses:</u>

Drop shipping a product: This is when you are able to negotiate a deal with a manufacturer and have them send the products to your customer directly. It's great because you don't have to hold any inventory. But, there are downsides also.

White labeling a product from Alibaba: This is when you find a product on a website like Alibaba and sell it under your brand name. This way, you don't have a design a product from scratch. You just gotta find one to sell and differentiate your marketing.

Designing your own product: It's a bit more complicated, but you can design your own prototype, buy a minimum order quantity, and sell it. I wouldn't say this is the fastest route, but it can create a solid business.

Selling on TeeSpring: Technically, this is a physical product that you're selling, but thankfully, it's all "print on demand" so you don't need to hold inventory. You just need to invest in high quality designs and market your products. You can sell others types as well like leggings, hats, or dress socks.

<u>The Best Type of Digital Nomad Business</u>

Personally, I think the best type of digital nomad business is to become an expert using a MAJOR content hub. This could be a:

- **YouTube channel:** Put out educational videos on a specific topic. You can use this to build a fanbase

- **Podcast:** Start a podcast where you interview guests and you share their expertise with the world.

- **Blog:** Start a blog where you write articles to attract an audience .

The great thing about an "expert" business model is that you can begin with one of the above content hubs for FREE and then use it to engage in things like affiliate marketing, where you sell other people's products online. It's like magic income.

You can also branch out and make money through online ads, sponsorships, and promotional packages. Then, you can further branch out by writing ebooks, putting together courses, and offering your services on a freelance basis.

Basically, the expert business model is all about creating a STRONG foundation that you can monetize in **multiple** ways. This way, you have many different residual income streams, and you can also sell your own time on top of that. You can sell your time through freelancing or online coaching. If this sounds interesting to you, then I think you'll like my course showing you exactly how to become a digital nomad.

(https://www.salvadorbriggman.com/digitalnomad)

Now that you are familiar with how to earn money as a freelancer and you have an idea of a few easy businesses that you can start, I want to begin to discuss the tax and legal implications of becoming a digital nomad. I know that this is kinda boring, but it's very important. While it might suck the fun out of planning your travels, having a firm grasp of the next chapter will make sure that you stay out of trouble. It is perfectly legal to travel the world, make money, and enjoy life. Just make sure that you play it by the book so that you can avoid any issues with your home country.

CHAPTER 7:

The Legality of Being a Digital Nomad & Tax Implications

You want to be a digital nomad, but you wanna do it by the book.

You don't want to end up in trouble with tax authorities or get hauled into a foreign jail and have to get your friends or family to go bail you out.

If you've made it this far in the book, then you probably find the idea of being a digital nomad attractive, but there are still some missing pieces of the puzzle. How the heck do you file your taxes? What are the legal implications of being location-independent?

As a business owner, I am hyper-vigilant about paying my taxes. I've received legal and tax advice before on business matters on multiple occasions. I believe that being informed about how the law works is the best insurance out there.

I am not an accountant or lawyer, so this is not legal or tax advice. It is my opinion. I recommend consulting both an accountant and a lawyer to properly guide you. What follows is my experience as a digital nomad, and some tips/advice that I'd like to pass on to you! It is by no means comprehensive. It's simply meant to get your toes wet.

Here's How Taxes Work

Let's start with the tax implications of being a digital nomad and earning money as you travel. No one likes taxes, but they do allow our governments to function properly.

When it comes to taxes, we're usually referring to:

- State and Local income taxes

- Federal income taxes

- Possibly self-employment tax

Naturally, these tax regulations will vary from **country to country** and **state to state.** For example, in Massachusetts, there is a 5% income tax on salaries, wages, tips, and commissions. However, in Florida, there is **NO** state income tax.

Your state and local taxes will be tied to where your permanent legal residence is. When it comes to the United States, all citizens must be a resident of a state for tax purposes. Typically, this is determined by:

- Where you're registered to vote

- Where you lived most of the year

- Where your mail goes

- Your state driver license issuer.

When you are abroad, if you are still a United States citizen, you will still pay state income taxes on a federal level. You may also need to file a state return.

According to USExpatTaxHelp.com, "If you are a US Citizen or resident alien living abroad not only do you have to ensure you file an income tax return with the IRS each year if you meet the minimum filing requirements, you may have to file a state tax return."

I would probably look up the state you are from and see what the minimum filing requirements are for filing a state return. When you are searching online, I would recommend using the keyword "expat." To give you an example, I'll list the requirements for Massachusetts, "Everyone whose Massachusetts gross income is $8,000 or more must file a Massachusetts personal income tax return."

This means that even if you were living abroad and making a normal income, you'd at the very least have to file your taxes in the state. How much you paid would be a different matter that you'd need to discuss with an accountant. In most cases, Digital Nomads are usually traveling for only part of the year and returning home occasionally. I would think about how long you want to travel and how often you will be back. Depending on how long you are away, you may need to track how often you're home. You might need to determine if you're a part-time resident, or if you're a non-resident.

What About Expat Taxes?

Now, things get a bit trickier if you consider yourself an expat instead of a digital nomad. As an expat, you're basically living overseas for good.

According to MyExpatTaxes, "Most expats do not pay US taxes because of the Foreign Earned Income Exclusion or Foreign Tax Credit benefits. However, expats still need to file taxes annually, even if they do not owe any taxes to the IRS. This holds true for the massive number of US expats that have gross worldwide income over the filing threshold."

In addition, expats may be working at a company that is based outside of the United States. They may have a foreign bank account and residence. Even if you don't end up paying US taxes as an expat, you will still need to report your income. Discussing Expat taxes goes beyond the scope of this chapter. It will also require consulting an accountant.

With this chapter, we are focusing on digital nomads who are traveling a couple of months at a time, and plan to continue to come back to the USA. When you transition into the expat category, you then have to start thinking about things like taxes that you may owe to foreign governments (if you're living abroad).

Foreign Earned Income Exclusion

There is something known as the foreign earned income exclusion, where you can exclude up to $100k of income earned abroad as long as these conditions are met:

- **Physical Presence Test:** You must live and work outside the USA for at least 330 days of any 365-day period.

- **Bona Fide Residence Test:** You must be living and working in a foreign country for an entire calendar year.

Again, this is for those hardcore nomads who are basically expats and do not plan on returning to the USA very much at all. You can learn more about the foreign earned income exclusion at TaxesForExpats.com.

Do You Pay Taxes to Foreign Governments?

This will depend on if you are sourcing income from those countries, if you're employed there, what your visa status is, and the laws of that particular country.

In addition, if you are setting up a business operation abroad, where you're dealing with inventory, paying suppliers, and making money, then you may need to look more closely into the local rules and regulations. For the average nomad who's just gone for 6 months bouncing around the globe and is working from their laptop, chances are you won't have to pay taxes, especially if your income sources are all online and not from local businesses.

What All This Means For YOU

For the average digital nomad who is traveling for 6 – 8 months, is visiting different countries, and is working from their laptop, this means that:

- You still must file and pay state/local taxes if you're in a state that requires this

- You still must file and pay federal taxes

- You may or may not need to pay self-employment taxes depending on your job status.

Remember, there are many different types of digital nomads. Some are freelancers (aka self-employed). Others are working for a company in a location-independent fashion. And, there are those like me, who have a business entity. By the way, even if you are a freelancer, I would recommend having a business entity, like an LLC or Limited Liability Company to shield yourself from legal liability.

Visas and Legal Issues

Phew, so we covered the basic taxes you'll have to consider as a digital nomad. Now, let's dive into the visas and legal issues you should be aware of.

The visa laws vary in two ways:

- Your home country residence

- The country you are visiting

As a US resident, there are countries that are more friendly to me than others. As a resident of another country, you need to check the visa laws for the country you're visiting.

In general, most digital nomads will use the following visas:

- **Tourist visa:** Varies by country, but usually 30 – 90 days for US citizens. You can typically extend it or do a "visa run" and re-enter the country to get your passport stamped again.

- **Immigration/naturalization:** This is more for expats. If you're intending on living in a foreign country for a long time, you'll want to look into this.

- **Student visas:** If you want to learn a language or take other credible education while abroad, you could consider this option.

- **Work or Business Visa:** If you're planning on doing things like attending business meetings, buying/ investing, consulting, etc.

In my travels, the tourist visa is definitely the most popular, however I also see some who are doing the education visa. The main thing with this type of visa is that you adhere to the requirements.

For example, in Thailand, you can get an education visa, but you must:

"Have been accepted on a full-time educational course, training program, or internship in Thailand. The school and course must be recognized by the Thai Government and the course must require students to attend classes for at least 100 hours for every 90-days; this roughly amounts to 8-10 hours per week." – (ImmigrationBangkok.com)

One creative way to fulfill this requirement would be to learn the Thai language, or take Muay Thai classes. Just remember that you're committing to that course of action for a good amount of time, so you can't always be traveling.

You can also look into some countries that have alternative visa options for digital nomads. For example, at the time of writing, Malaysia has a 1-year tourist visa!

Legalities of Starting a Business As a Nomad

Okay – so, you could start a business in the United States OR one abroad, in another country.

Let me just knock this out of the way and say that setting up a business in another country goes beyond the scope of this chapter, but that there is a great guide on the pros and cons of this at TaxesForExpats.com.

One line that stood out to me is:

"One of the largest benefits to operating an overseas corporation is that of tax deferral. You can use tax-deferred money to generate extra profits by re-investing the tax savings amount into the corporation. This practice can produce enough extra income to equal – and possibly surpass – the amount in taxes which would be owed." – (TaxesForExpats.com)

So, you won't get away with not paying taxes if you are a US citizen, but you could defer those taxes it appears with a foreign corporation.

When it comes to a business within the United States, you have a few different options:

- **Sole Proprietor:** What you are by default in the eyes of the law if you're a freelancer.

- **Limited Liability Company:** This offers some legal protection by making it so that your own assets and your company's are different. If someone sues your company, they can't get to your personal assets (though you must follow rules to establish this separation).

- **S Corporation:** These are taxed differently than LLCs, though as an LLC you can elect to be taxed as an S corporation.

- **C Corporation:** These typically are reserved for larger companies with multiple stockholders and potential investors. They require you to pay corporate tax and taxes after you distribute, so double taxes. There is definitely more separation of assets though from the company and the founder.

For the average digital nomad, you'd probably be most interested in a single-member LLC or an S corporation. There are tax savings to be had depending on which you choose.

As a single member LLC, the income generated passes through to you as the individual and you pay regular income taxes and self-employment taxes. As a S Corporation, you are an employee of the company and thus must set up a payroll system. However, you don't have to pay self-employment tax.

Having a corporate entity will help to shield you should any of your customers ever decide to sue you. It is also good business practice to:

- Have a company credit/debit card to track company expenses

- Have a separate company bank account

- Have an EIN number to track company revenue to establish the corporate veil

Why You Should Have a Business

Even if you're a freelancer, this is why you should have a business.

Aside from the things I mentioned in the last section, business owners get considerable benefits. Let's just say that you don't know how to operate a business. You don't know anything about tracking expenses.

Individual A: You don't know anything about business

You earn $75,000.

You pay taxes on this number, and let's assume it's about $22,500 in taxes (or 30%).

You end up with $52,500 of after-tax income at the end of the year.

Individual B: You are educated about business

Now, let's factor in what would happen if you knew how to properly track your expenses, income, and operate as a business.

You earn $75,000.

You have $15,000 in tracked expenses using software like QuickBooks or even just Excel.

Therefore, your "taxable income" is $60,000. You pay $18,000 in taxes (or 30%)

You end up with $57,000 at the end of the year.

In scenario A, you ended up with $52,500 in after-tax income. In scenario B, you ended up with $57,000 in after-tax income. There are no differences in lifestyle, income, or amount spent between these two people. In the eyes of the government, one is simply claiming some of their expenses as business expenses. Because they are "business expenses," they can be subtracted from that individual's taxable income to arrive at a lowered taxable income.

When compared, this is a difference of $4,500. You basically saved yourself this money.

Pretty neat, huh?

You could save that money, put into the stock market, go partying, or pay for a couple of flights around the world. Person A and Person B are the same people. One is just paying more taxes because they don't know anything about business.

The Laws Are In Your Favor

In general, the laws are in your favor as a business owner.

For example, with the recent paycheck protection program, you could get considerable free money just by virtue of being a business owner. I hope that this shows you why it's so freakin' important to become educated about these things. That's really my passion. I want to help you do this whole digital nomad thing, but in a smarter way.

When I was younger, I was shocked to discover just how different the laws are for business owners as compared to normal individuals. I learned about the difference between investment income and earned income. I read up on the tax benefits of owning real estate. Business owners have a whole set of special privileges, like being able to write off losses so that they don't have to pay taxes on future income. Through the use of corporate entities, taxes, and the business legal framework, America encourages entrepreneurs to take risks. It's all spelled out in black and white.

When I first learned this, it was unsettling. The average individual who doesn't understand our legal or tax system can feel left out. It's like the rules were written out of your favor. Suddenly, you begin to realize why entrepreneurship is the largest source of wealth creation for our society. It's because it's easier to get rich through a successful business than by earning a big salary. Just look at the newest millionaires and billionaires who started from nothing. Almost all of them started their own company or were in the early stages of a fast-growing startup.

I came to realize that it's easier to swim with the tide than against it. Even as an individual freelancer, or a small business owner, you can use these laws to your favor. Not only can things like corporate entities grant you legal protection and prevent the seizure of your assets, but they can also help you to pay less taxes. With more money in your pocket, you can invest in your future and grow your income faster.

CHAPTER 8:

Best Digital Nomad Cities and Communities

Traveling is hella' fun!

It's even more fun when you meet cool people throughout your journey.

While "living the laptop lifestyle" used to be a pipe dream, now it's actually a reality. You don't have to be a scam artist in order to live in an exotic location. There are tons of work at home jobs which will lead you to a life of total location independence.

If you want to go to the hub of tech startups, you go to **Silicon Valley.**

If you wanna become an actress or movie star, you go to **Hollywood.**

If you wanna become a digital nomad.... where should you go?

That's what this chapter is designed to answer. I'll give you the list in a no-nonsense fashion so that you can start your planning. It's really exciting to venture out and travel the world, but just remember to take care of your physical and mental health while you do so.

Also, the cities that I find to be the best may differ from your preferences, so be sure to check out a website like Nomadlist, which allows you filter the top cities for nomads based on your cost preferences.

I would strongly recommend deciding on the region of the world you'd like to live in, before choosing the destination city. This will simplify a lot of your travel planning. You'll have a clear sense of the side trips you can take and the surrounding countries that are waiting to be discovered. I made this mistake the hard way.

During my first 8-month travel binge, I first went to Peru for a month, then to Spain, then to the USA, then to Colombia, then back to the USA, and then to Thailand and the rest of Southeast Asia. I had to keep traveling back to the USA for family obligations. Looking back, I was bouncing around the globe. Had I confined my travels to one region of the world, I would have had an easier time with my planning. Granted, I did have a lot of fun going all over.

Anyway, let's jump into the best digital nomad cities and the top digital nomad communities!

Chiang Mai, Thailand – Southeast Asia

Chiang Mai is nestled in the mountains of Thailand and is surrounded by nature, beautiful temples, and cute wild animals, like Elephants. It's extremely safe, affordable, and you'll meet lots of other Westerners (along with locals).

To me, what stood out in Chiang Mai was its strong digital nomad hub, with a myriad of coworking spaces, cafes, and offices with good WIFI. There are many established coworking spaces that allow you to get your work done in a comfortable air-conditioned environment. I would also visit quaint little cafes to do my writing work. It's very easy to get a SIM card for your phone in Thailand, so even if there's no WIFI at a café, you'll never have to be without internet.

For the most part, you can decide to live in the Old City or the New City or Nimmanhaemin. I lived in both for a short period of time.

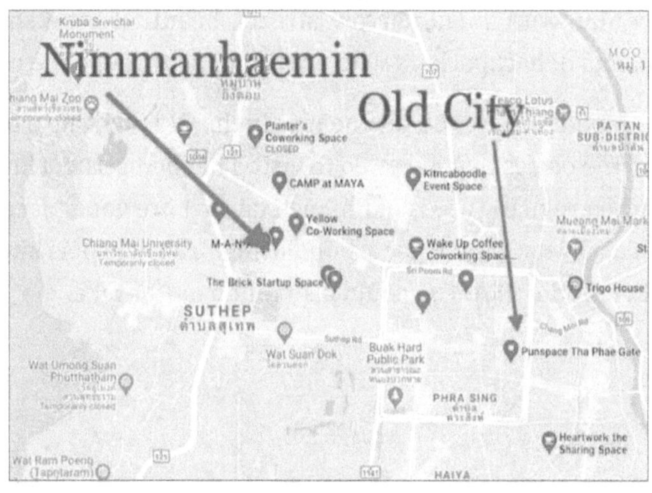

There are a lot of night markets all over the city, cheap food places, and there are some fun going out places in Old City where you might meet other young travelers. If you're not interested in "going out," then there are still tons of options available for you. You won't have trouble making friends, because there are also lots of great activities like yoga and meditation.

What struck me about Nimmanhaemin was its upper-class feel. You'll find beautiful malls, food courts, restaurants, classy rooftop bars, and western-style cafes that serve things like delicious iced coffee. This area of the city is a bit more expensive to stay in, but if you're worried about having access to modern amenities it's a good choice. Basically, a lot of the wealthier tourists stay here. You might feel a little bit of culture shock initially, but I assure you that this is a very safe area of the world.

At first, I was very hesitant about staying in the Old City, but I couldn't have been more wrong. I arrived in Chiang Mai right around New Year's Eve, because I wanted to see all the beautiful lanterns floating in the sky. I wanted to make sure that I had good accommodations, given all the festivities. I had a great time, but the week after New Year's, I moved into an Airbnb that was in the Old City, and oh man, it was such a different feel. The Old City is what you might picture when you think of Chiang Mai, with small narrow streets, beautiful little shops and cafes, and lots of backpackers who are traveling through the region.

My accommodations were a lot cheaper in the Old City, and a bit closer to some of the places that I wanted to visit. That being said, I loved both areas. There are many areas of Chiang Mai that are good places to call home. It's also very easy to get around using Grab, which is kind of like Uber or Lyft in the USA. You could also rent a motor bike.

Chiang Mai itself does not have a beach, but you can easily go to some of the neighboring cities in Thailand to find one. One of the great things about Chiang Mai is that because you're in the center of South East Asia, you can travel all around to places like Cambodia, Vietnam, or across the water to the Philippines. There are also some great places within Thailand, like Phuket, Krabi, or Pattaya, but they are more tourist centric.

You can stay in the city of Chiang Mai or go on a weekend getaway to a beach, for the cost of a plane ticket, which is about $50 – $100 depending on the timing. Not bad at all! The very first time that I visited Thailand, I stayed in Phuket for about 3 weeks. I was a young guy, so I was mostly interested in partying the night away with friends and people that I met along the way.

In recent years Phuket has certainly become more expensive, but it's still a great beach destination. There are different areas of the island depending on the type of vacation-goer that you are. Just like with other locations in Thailand, there is something for everyone. Phuket is also a great destination for families. There are many luxury-style resorts that you can choose from.

Resources for Chiang Mai:

Best Coworking Spaces in Chiang Mai

- https://digitaltourist.co/best-coworking-spaces-chiang-mai/

Best Night Markets in Chiang Mai

- http://www.chiangmai.bangkok.com/shopping/5-must-visit-markets-in-chiang-mai.htm

Best Temples in Chiang Mai

- http://www.chiangmai.bangkok.com/top10-best-temples.htm

$50 off Airbnb Booking

- http://www.salvadorbriggman.com/airbnb

Videos on Chiang Mai:

New Years Eve Lanterns in Chiang Mai, Thailand

- https://youtu.be/hgzl6E0ezF4

Hug Elephant Sanctuary in Chiang Mai, Thailand

- https://youtu.be/p7AfQA0QTbw

Temples in Chiang Mai, Thailand

- https://youtu.be/34F95eAIr90

Krabi

- https://www.youtube.com/watch?v=VkTRXLQsW4g

Medellin, Colombia – South America

I've said this once, and I'll say it again. Medellin is the up and coming digital nomad hot spot. It's called the "land of eternal springtime" for a reason. The weather is beautiful. It's very easy to get around using Uber or taxis, and there are lot of things to do like horseback riding, paragliding, hiking, and modern gym facilities.

The food is very affordable outside of the touristy areas and it's cheap living if you want to get an Airbnb. I stayed in El Poblado the first time that I was there in an Airbnb. In the central area, there are coworking spaces, co-living spaces, and a lot of other nomads. There are also many westerners just traveling for fun.

What stood out in my mind about Medellin was how, compared to many other cities that I had visited in Lain America, there was much more of a welcoming vibe for foreigners. I actually met other people from the United States that were digital nomads. It was very easy to find fun activities to do from Airbnb experiences and by browsing around online. That's how I got connected with a great photographer there to take some killer photos for my Instagram. It's also how I found out about cool things like paragliding, where you can get the sensation of floating over the city and doing the Comuna 13 Graffiti Tour. In addition, I did a helicopter tour all around Medellin, which was amazing. At night, there are many modern restaurants to eat at, and familiar western-style joints. You can also go more of the authentic route. It's really up to you.

The only negative that I spotted with Medellin was that you do need to know basic Spanish to get around. While people do speak English, Spanish will certainly help you if you ever get lost or you want to ask someone a question. For the most part, Uber drivers don't speak much English, so if you ever need to direct someone more specifically, Spanish helps. There were also situations, like trying to get a SIM card, when knowing some Spanish aided me a great deal. The other frustration that I had with Colombia was getting a SIM card. I had to visit a few places until I found one (Claro) that would give me a SIM as a tourist. It was annoying. Then, I could only top up 2 gigabytes at a time. I just wanted to buy a 10-gigabyte internet package, but that wasn't available.

Lastly, for the most part, I felt safe in the city during the daytime and at night, but there are some not so great section of the city. Be careful, especially if you are traveling alone. Don't be too flashy. In my experience, most of the time, the people who will try to steal things from you will be on a motor bike (for a quick getaway). So, if you're walking along the side of the road alone at night, or in a sketchy area with people on motor bikes, then be more vigilant. You don't want to run into any issues.

Resources for Medellin:

Medellin Guru (love this site)

- https://medellinguru.com/

Best Medellin Coworking Spaces

- https://wifitribe.co/blog/medellin-coworking-spaces/

Overview to Living in Medellin

- https://clairesitchyfeet.com/medellin-digital-nomad/

Fun things to do!

- https://www.nomadicmatt.com/travel-blogs/ultimate-list-medellin/

Videos on Medellin:

Paragliding in Medellin, Colombia

- https://www.youtube.com/watch?v=kwMCzJBj-mk

Top Fun Things to Do in Medellin, Colombia

- https://www.youtube.com/watch?v=AH2Lzr-aMdw

Nightlife in Medellin, Colombia

- https://www.youtube.com/watch?v=R7QbasyD9Aw

Canggu, Bali – Indonesia/Lower SEA

It goes without saying that Bali has to be on the list, even though there are some very expensive areas of it. At this point, Bali is basically a brand name.

There are many regions of Bali, but Canggu is on the south coast of the Indonesian island. It has lots of pretty dope rice paddies and beaches. There are some sick waves for surfers, if you're into that kinda thing.

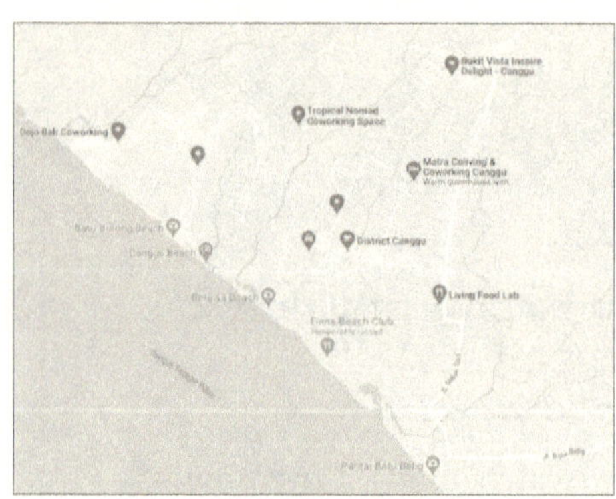

In Canggu, there are a lot of younger people and it's very safe. There are party areas and also areas that are quieter. It's up to you. Of course, there are lots of great co-working spaces. The food is relatively cheap.

Canggu isn't the only area to stay in. There are quite a few in the south of Bali, like Ubud, Kuta, etc.

One thing that you may want to be aware of is the rainy season, as that may determine how long you spend in Bali. Most areas in Southeast Asia have an optimal time to visit.

Be aware that the costs to live in Bali are increasing.

"As long as you have money, finding a place to stay in Bali is easy. Airbnb has the most options for places to rent. You'll struggle to find a nice place for under $800 a month. If your budget is $1,000+ for living in Bali, you'll have plenty of choice." – Hobo With a Laptop

Resources:

The BEST Coworking in Bali

- https://thehoneycombers.com/bali/coworking-spaces-bali-work-remotely/

Best Places Throughout Bali

- https://santorinidave.com/best-places-bali

Good Guide on Bali

- https://hobowithalaptop.com/digital-nomad-bali-guide

Lisbon, Portugal – Europe

Lisbon is becoming a more attractive location for digital nomads worldwide, particularly if you wanna set down your roots in Europe. It's a lot more affordable than other places like Madrid.

The biggest plus is probably the weather. It's very nice most of the year. There is reliable, fast wifi and the standard of living is a bit cheaper than other areas of Europe. It's relatively safe too. One of the other pluses is the 90-day visa for Americans. Most other countries are around 30.

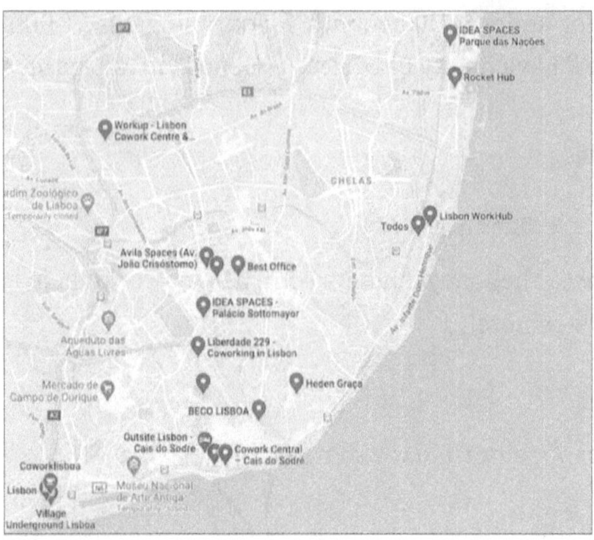

There are lots of cafes, coworking spaces, and many day trips that you can make from the city. Since you're in Europe, a lot of other epic cities are only a plane ticket away. It makes traveling a lot easier if you wanna check some cities off the bucket list.

In terms of day trips, you can go to the beach, check out some castles, or visit wineries and vineyards.

Resources:

Best Lisbon Coworking Spaces

- https://www.portugalist.com/best-coworking-spaces-lisbon/

A good Guide on Lisbon

- https://www.outsite.co/blog/digital-nomad-guide-to-lisbon-portugal

Day Trips From Lisbon

- https://www.thecrazytourist.com/15-best-day-trips-lisbon/

Find a Place in Lisbon

- http://www.salvadorbriggman.com/airbnb

Budapest, Hungary – Central/Eastern Europe

This city is in Central/Eastern Europe and is another great spot for location independent workers who want to reside in this area of the world. As you can see below, it is bordered by Ukraine, Romania, Austria, Serbia, and more.

One of the things that I like to think about when choosing my digital nomad location is the surrounding travel areas. So, if you wanted to make a journey of going to different Eastern European countries to get a feel for them, then Hungary might be a great home base! They speak Hungarian, of course.

There are numerous coworking spaces in the city which you can choose from to work on your various projects. You can see a snapshot of them below.

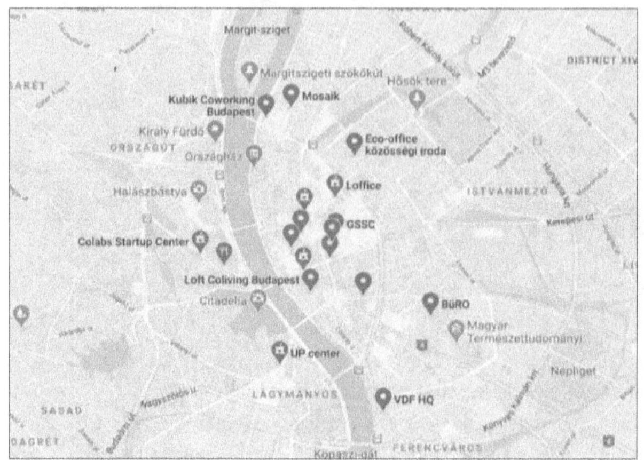

One of the things that you should keep in mind if you'd like to live here is that the weather is a bit on the colder side in the winter months and hot in July. Basically, the seasons you might be used to if you live in the North East USA. There does seem to be a bit of a homelessness problem, but that is true of many major cities.

You don't need a car to get around. The food is pretty cheap, and many people do speak English. There are many cafes, coworking spaces, and restaurants to enjoy. This seems like a great option if you don't want to go somewhere too exotic, but also want beautiful architecture and fun things to do.

Resources:

Where to stay for Nomads

- https://micropreneur.life/life-in-budapest-for-digital-nomads/

Coworking Spaces in Budapest

- https://nomadsecrets.com/budapests-best-coworking-spaces/

- https://www.christhefreelancer.com/budapest-for-digital-nomads/

Prague – Central Europe

Prague is a little bit north of Budapest. It's bordered by Poland, Germany, Austria, and Slovakia. It's the capital of the Czech Republic.

Digital nomads tend to find this location appealing for its relatively cheap living and decent English mastery. You can walk along the

riverside, get drinks from boat bars, take in incredible views, and enjoy the various beer gardens.

There is also an active Expat scene in Prague, so you won't have too much trouble meeting other people if you put yourself out there. There are meetups and groups designed for this. It's pretty safe, especially for women.

No doubt, the architecture is beautiful. Like most European cities, you will be able to find coworking spaces to suit your needs. If you enjoy history, you'll probably like what this city has to offer.

Resources:

Great guide on Prague

- https://digitalnomadlove.com/2018/08/26/10-reasons-why-prague-is-heaven-for-digital-nomads/

Best areas to live in

- https://digitalnomadgirls.com/digital-nomad-girls-guide-prague/

Coworking Spaces in Prague

- https://www.eustartups.com/2017/03/overview-of-the-best-coworking-spaces-in-prague/

Book a place in Prague

- http://www.salvadorbriggman.com/airbnb

Belgrade, Serbia – Central/Eastern Europe

Belgrade is a bit more south than Prague, which certainly influences its weather. You'll find that it's bordered by Romania, Hungary, Bulgaria, and a few others.

Now, in my opinion, this is a bit newer on the map when it comes to location independent workers. In fact, there is a new tax incentive created by the government, which says "Serbia plans 0% tax for digital nomads starting 2020 for up to 90 days." – NomadNotMad.

Personally, I'm not sure how that really impacts things, because it's pretty hard for Serbia to identify that you're earning income in the country, if your bank accounts are in another country, you're not working for a Serbian company, AND all your work is online.

Regardless, it's a nice idea. Serbia is becoming more attractive due to the great cost of living. It's one of the cheaper countries within Europe. If you're into it, there is also a pretty good night life, I hear. Unfortunately, since it's newer to the scene, there isn't as much of a digital nomad community. You might be better off tapping into the expat community.

One of the things I like about this country is that you have up to 90 days with the visa. Also, there are some great day trips that you can do.

Resources:

Some good coworking spaces in Belgrade

- https://www.webworktravel.com/digital-nomad-belgrade/

A good review of life in Belgrade

- https://www.christhefreelancer.com/belgrade-for-digital-nomads/

Book your room in Belgrade

- http://www.salvadorbriggman.com/airbnb

Not gonna lie, when I first heard about it, I wasn't sure if Georgia was a part of Asia or in the middle east. It's situated on the Black Sea and is right above Turkey.

One of the MAJOR wins about Georgia is that you can stay in the country for 365 days without a visa, if you're a US citizen. That's, like unheard of.

It's a pretty good cost of living, like most of the cities on this list. There is affordable transportation, decent food, and oddly the culture is a mix of Eastern European, Middle Eastern, and Asian.

I think one of the other attractive parts of Georgia is that it's situated pretty close to Russia, Turkey, and other Eastern European countries. There are also some very friendly business/tax laws.

Resources:

Cost of living and food

- https://theculturetrip.com/europe/georgia/articles/move-georgia-youre-digital-nomad/

Taxes for Nomads, etc.

- https://nomadflag.com/tbilisi-georgia/#Tax-For-Nomads-Expats

Book a place in Georgia

- http://www.salvadorbriggman.com/airbnb

Tallinn, Estonia

Tallinn is a quaint little town that's located way up north by Finland and Sweden. You might not have considered this location, but it might be the next location for digital nomads.

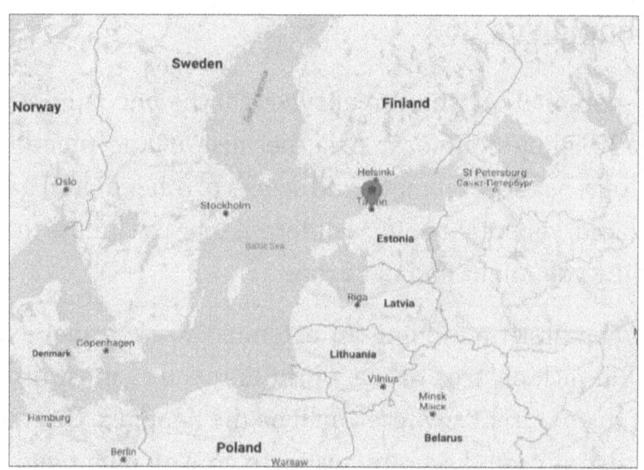

It's a very highly advanced online society. There are even rules for digital nomads. "Estonia has just announced the first official visa for digital nomads. The permit will entitle nomads to 365 days of working in Estonia, including 90 days' travel in the Schengen area." – The Guardian.

It has the second fastest public WIFI in the world. A lot of programmers and coders live here. It's an affordable place to live at the time of writing. It's a small, safe city. One of the downsides are the harsh winters. Oh boy, you can only imagine, considering it's so north. There is a mix of Estonian and Russian speaking individuals.

Resources:

Good guide on Estonia

- https://micropreneur.life/life-in-tallinn-for-digital-nomads/

Another decent review

- https://www.odenventures.com/digital-nomad-review-tallinn-estonia/

Book a place in Tallinn

- http://www.salvadorbriggman.com/airbnb

<u>Where Should You Go?</u>

It's a very personal question to answer. On the one hand, I think you would really enjoy Southeast Asia, because of the plentiful budget travel options, beautiful climate, and scores of other digital nomads. On the other hand, you might enjoy a different vibe or climate that's closer to something you might find in Europe.

If this is your first time doing an extended work/travel experience, then I would pick an area of the world that you're most drawn to. At the end of the day, that's where you'll be the happiest. Our heart takes us places that our mind secretly wants to go. You might end up loving the location or hating it. Either way, you'll at least get out of fantasy and into reality.

After spending a very long and hard year working in New York City, I was determined to travel for an extended period of time. I was following this one travel blogger who was raving about Peru, specifically Cusco. I was reading articles from this guy for months, and he really sold me on the country and the experience. So, my first destination in my 8-month long travel binge was Peru. I was so excited. I was ready to have an adventure.

I was happy for about a week, and then depression set in. While Peru was cool, it wasn't a place that I would want to stay for longer than two weeks. I just didn't enjoy it. I didn't like the culture as much as I thought I would. I loved seeing Machu Picchu, meeting Alpacas, and doing some outdoor activities. However, as a solo traveler, it was very lonely. I think if I had gone with friends or a group, it would have been much better. Keep in mind, I have traveled solo to other countries in Latin/South America like Colombia and El Salvador.

What I came to realize was that this "travel expert" was wrong. Well, not wrong per se, but wrong for me. It's the same way that you might end up watching and **hating** a movie that your friend recommends. Just because someone else likes something and recommends it, does not mean that it will be a good experience for you. Always take recommendations with a grain of salt.

On that note, when it comes to digital nomad locations, if you would like some advice outside of my own then I'd check out these digital nomad communities around the web:

1. Nomad List

2. Digital Nomad Girls on Facebook

3. Digital Nomad Forum on Facebook

4. Meetup.com

5. Reddit Nomad

Now that you're familiar with some of the top countries, cities, and locations to visit on your travels, I want to start to get into the lifestyle component of being a digital nomad. Remember the formula we talked about? Digital Nomad Success = Income + Location + Lifestyle. You can have the first two, but if you're not aware of what the lifestyle is like, then you might end up unhappy or falling into depression, like I did at different points in time. The next chapter will introduce you to the lifestyle, and some critical things that you should know before you take the plunge.

CHAPTER 9:

Digital Nomad Lifestyle
Tips for Mental Health and Happiness

When you're traveling as a digital nomad, your lifestyle isn't always at the top of your mind. You're too focused on earning money, discovering cool places around the world, and making friends. However, if you aren't aware of some of the advice that I'll share in this chapter, you might end up unhappy, frustrated, and confused as to why you feel this way. I went through a mini-depression period through my own travels.

If you wanna make sure that your travels are as smooth as possible, then I think you'll like some of the advice that I'll share in this chapter. These are practical ways to improve your lifestyle, take care of your mental health, and boost your happiness while traveling.

Create a Work-Life Balance

Haha – wow. I did a really bad job of this when I was traveling for the first time.

I couldn't find a balance between my career and doing fun things while traveling. I have a very extreme personality, and I'm usually "all in" or "all out" when it comes to projects. What ended up happening was… in the beginning of my travels, I was working every day, going to the gym, and maintaining my usual routine. Only, I wasn't leaving enough time to explore or have adventures.

It left me feeling miserable, and like a great opportunity was passing me by. Why should I be in an air-conditioned room, staring at a computer screen, when I could be out there doing cool sh*t!?!?

After I had this realization, I kind of flipped to the other side, where I was spending 80% of my time having fun, and only 20% on work. It got pretty bad, and I fell behind. I basically didn't make any progress career-wise and in some ways, even went backwards a few steps.

Work life balance is crucial for your career, but it's also important for your mental health and well-being. When I started to have more fun, I was certainly having a good time, but I could feel myself becoming **less confident.**

My confidence comes from completing projects, doing good work, kicking ass, and taking names. When I'm not doing those things, I feel like my life is stagnant. I don't feel confident about my future.

It will be hard to have work-life balance when you're traveling, so **be aware of this.**

Traveling is literally a part-time job. You have to figure out where you'll be going, what you'll be doing, what the visa requirements are, and a whole host of other things. The more itinerary planning you can do ahead of time, the easier it will be to just enjoy. That brings me to my next point!

Know What Makes You Happy

It doesn't matter what age you are. You're still getting to know yourself. But, up until this point, you should have some idea of what makes you happy.

In a later point, I'll recommend starting a travel journal. In your first few pages, you should take an assessment of your life and write out a few things that make you happy. You can reference this later when you feel down and see if you're continuing to participate in those things.

Some people enjoy waking up early and going on a 7-hour bus ride to see a natural phenomenon, like a waterfall. Other people would rather spend that time relaxing on the beach. The only difference is your personality.

When you're traveling alone and seeing other people do things, like go hiking or ATVing, there is a big temptation to feel the need to join along. Sometimes, this can be fun. Other times, it can be draining.

There's no other way to say it. Know what makes you happy. This will save you a lot of headache down the road.

Whenever I violated this principle, I was miserable. For example, I prefer living in cities as opposed to rural areas. After a few days in a rural area, I start feeling antsy. I don't like the slower pace of life. It starts to weigh on my mood.

I sold myself on the idea that being in Peru for a month, specifically Cusco and the surrounding areas, would be a good idea. I could go hiking, experience nature, and live in a quaint little town. Man, was that a bad choice.

It was only once I got back to a big city that I breathed a sigh of relief. It was like I was home again. My depression lifted and I was 10x happier.

Know what's going to put a smile on your face.

Incorporate Meditation Into Your Routine

THIS IS A MUST!

If you have never meditated before or aren't familiar with the concept of mindfulness, take a second to check out my book, Unlocking Human Potential on Amazon.

Meditation is important because it grounds you in the present moment. It eliminates your worries about the future or your negative thoughts about the past.

This simple exercise can help to dramatically alleviate your feelings of anxiety. It will allow you to connect with yourself in a deeper way that you have never thought possible. Even 15 minute a day will have a profound effect over time.

We all suffer from moment of brain fog, mental overwhelm, and being on autopilot. The easiest way to clear away these problems is through meditation. A simple meditation routine can take the form of a 20-minute session in the morning before you begin the day, or at night if you find that you can't turn off your problem-solving brain.

If you need help and guidance, you can always reach out to me for some extra educational content. I love seeing new people embracing this centuries-old exercise to calm their emotions and promote well-being.

Journal and Catalogue Your Travels

I am so happy that I kept a travel journal. This is an invaluable resource. You can use it to do a few things:

- Remember experiences, thoughts, and good times throughout your journey

- Capture and track your emotions over the span of time

- Identify and fix negative patterns of thoughts, behaviors, or emotions

You don't need anything fancy. I have a black leather journal that I picked up on Amazon.

Make sure that you start the first few weeks with the habit of regularly writing in your journal. I would do it every 2-3 days, even if it was just for ten minutes at a time. There's a strong temptation to avoid writing in your journal or rationalize that you'll remember everything on your travels. Don't give in!

This journal is such a valuable resource for me. Not only did it crystalize my travels, but I can look back and see exactly how I **felt** in different regions of the world. I can go back into a memory and see exactly what I was thinking when something happened. It's an oddly intimate way of getting to know yourself.

Create a Friendship Maintenance Plan

I knew ahead of time that I was going to have trouble maintaining my existing friendships. I'm just not very good at that sort of thing. I picked the handful that mattered most to me and made sure to message them when I could. Only, sometimes I slipped up… and they let me know.

When you change the physical location that you're in, it makes it ten times harder to maintain relationships in your old location. You can't make new memories. You can only go into maintenance mode, reminisce about old events, and keep people as updated as you can.

Unfortunately, this is just part of travel. You have to leave parts of you behind in order to experience the world. You're never going to be able to fill everyone in on everything you've experienced, so pick a few friends you want to stay close with, and make sure to stay in touch.

Failure to do this can create feelings of loneliness. It can really harm your sense of wellbeing. I'd recommend doing a video chat at least every 2 months to try to keep up with existing relationships that you have.

Sometimes, having a friend see your face is all they (and you) need to re-connect. It can be as simple as that.

Put a Date on Your Travels Back Home

You might not have a family that demands time and attention, but I sure do.

If you plan to be traveling around the world, make sure that you're clear about when you're going to come home to see the family. Maybe this is during Thanksgiving and Christmas. It will depend on your family.

Having some pre-defined dates that I planned to be home made it a lot easier to relax family members who were concerned that I might be traveling for too long, or who were worried about my whereabouts. You might not care, but I'm an only child, so there is a lot more attention on me in my family.

There were times that I was out of contact for a couple weeks just because of the location I was in and my availability. If nothing else, send some emails. People want to hear from you. You could always use Whatsapp or a similar application to stay connected.

I'm not very good at communication all the time, so having those pre-defined dates on the calendar was a good solution for me. My family was less worried about the next time that they would have the chance to see me.

Learn Which Environments Suit Your Personality

You might already have a clear sense about this, but I didn't. Looking back, I wish I had changed up my living arrangements for certain cities. For example, rather than staying in an Airbnb in Cusco, Peru, I wish I had stayed in a hostel. This would have made socializing a lot easier and I would have been less lonely.

In other areas, like Cambodia, I didn't get much value out of staying in a hostel. I would have been just fine living in an Airbnb, because the nightlife was bountiful enough for me to socialize a bit on my own. I also wasn't staying there for very long.

As I stated before, I tend to like city environments more than the country. I do enjoy being in the country, but not for much more than a week. Then, I need to return to civilization. I was also traveling alone.

My most recent trip made me realize that sometimes, it is fun to travel with other people. There are certain environments where I would do that. Other countries, I'd rather explore on my own. You only learn that through trial and error.

Consider Travel Insurance

In order to minimize headaches, you could consider looking into getting travel insurance to cover major medical emergencies throughout your journey.

I talk a bit about this, along with tax and legal issues you might encounter, in my course called "How to Be a Digital Nomad – Achieve Location Independence."

Travel insurance has its upsides. If you're only going to be visiting somewhere for a short time, you can probably simply use the insurance that you buy when you book your airline ticket. If you're spending a longer time, then you may want to look into an alternative solution.

Use a VPN!

If you've never use a VPN before, it's basically a magical piece of software that you can install on your computer in seconds. You can use it to access the internet from ANYWHERE in the world.

That means, if you're accessing the internet from your laptop in Vietnam, you could fool the internet to think that you're accessing it from New York.

Why would you want to do that?

Because a lot of online services are tied to your home country, like Netflix, for example. Also, you'll get lots of weird search results and YouTube results sometimes in a foreign country.

Lastly, if you're accessing an application that you use frequently, that application may lock you out if they sense you're coming from a different location than normal. This can lead to massive headaches, especially if you can't authenticate using your cell phone.

I recommend looking into NordVPN, which is basically the gold standard of VPNs. They do a really good job of keeping their software robust, and they give you a lot of options from where you can access the internet.

Plan for Credit Card & Phone Issues

I actually didn't expect this to be an issue. I had contacted my bank before leaving for a long 7-month travel binge. But, it turned out to be a big issue, particularly when I was traveling in Latin America.

There were points in time where I couldn't call my bank, because it was the weekend, and my debit (and credit) cards weren't working. I didn't know what to do. I wish I had done something like buy pre-paid gift cards or buy Airbnb credit.

That's until I discovered Privacy.com, which is a great app that lets you create debit card numbers on the fly. You can basically make single-use cards. Any time my card wasn't working, I would just create a virtual privacy card and then it would work fine. The website basically works as an intermediary.

Another good idea would be to buy a burner phone that you can put your old sim card into. This way, if you need to get text messages, you can have them sent to your burner phone. Otherwise, what will end up happening is you'll try to log into key applications (like PayPal), only to find that you've been locked out and need to verify with your phone. Only you can't use your phone and you have a new sim card.

<u>I wanted to pull my hair out.</u>

Have a plan for the times when you will need to "authenticate using your phone." I would recommend, if possible, to use an Authenticator App, which usually is a possibility for social networks like Facebook. You just have to look into it. This way, you won't need to use your phone number.

<u>Consider Subletting Your Current Apartment</u>

If you already have an apartment with a yearlong lease, you might be able to sublet your apartment for a few months while you're traveling (depending on the agreement, of course). Should a friend or roommate be willing to help, you could even put your place up on Airbnb for short-term guests. This is a very common way to make some side income, without having to find a whole new renter who will commit to long sublease. It's also less sketchy than going on Craigslist.

Subletting is very common in New York City, where I'm based, and it can be a great way to supplement your income while abroad. It will take care of the fixed cost of your apartment and make it easier on you from a financial standpoint. If you want to try out the digital nomad lifestyle, subletting can also be an easy way to create a safety net so that you're not spending too much money while you're in another country.

Looking back, the only regret that I had when I went on my first digital nomad trek was that I didn't sublet my apartment. I was so new to the whole lifestyle, that I wasn't sure how to go about it. So, rather than dealing with the hassle, I just continued to pay rent, even though I wasn't living there. Thankfully, it was only for one month, but it was still a pretty sizable expense. When I did my calculations, I realized that

I could have actually saved money while traveling had I subleased my apartment. Hopefully, you can avoid this mistake that I made.

Pre-Schedule As Much Work As You Can

This assumes that you already have a business that's up and running, or that you're continuing to work for your employer in a remote fashion. Regardless, I would systematize all of the efforts that go into generating your primary revenue sources. This will take a huge load off your back. You'll be better organized while you're traveling. You'll just have to focus on the immediate tasks that you need to get done to avoid going into the red.

For me, I pre-scheduled blog posts and podcasts for the entire month that I was in Thailand. I also prioritized and decided on the action items that I could ignore on a daily basis and that I'd only check up on weekly. The next time I traveled I pre-scheduled all of my YouTube videos. This way, I didn't need to worry about finding good filming locations, or how I was going to lug around bulky expensive camera equipment. It saved me a lot of headaches.

Not only does pre-scheduling take a lot of worry out of the equation while you're traveling, but it also has the added benefit of freeing up time, so that you can work on other things while you're abroad. This can lead to starting new projects, trying out sports or activities, having a spiritual experience, or taking that time to finally write your book.

By the way, if you have a very service-oriented business, then you might want to consider hiring a virtual assistant or capable freelancer who can help you increase your work output. In this way, you'll become more of a manager and you can pre-schedule tasks for your worker.

Establish a Home Base.

This has been a very important part of all my trips. For my first trip to Thailand, rather than trying to plan out a bunch of stuff that I wanted to do before I had left for the country, I blocked off 3 weeks in Patong and 1 week in Bangkok.

I put my effort into establishing a lifestyle in these cities rather than plotting out a bunch of adventures before I got there. I spend the first two days figuring out:

- Where to do laundry

- Cheap places to eat regularly

- Different places I could travel from that location.

- Where I could get the best internet.

- A gym where I could workout.

Once I had this set, I then felt more comfortable taking day trips. Having these home bases allowed me to be more consistent with my work, because I wasn't thinking about a million things like where I was going to spend the night the next day or how I was going to get from point A to point B.

The next time I visited Thailand, I made Bangkok my home base. From there, I visited the beach town of Krabi, the mountains of Sapa, Vietnam, Ha Long Bay, the ancient temples in Cambodia, and the beautiful scenery in the Philippines. Everything was just a short flight away. If I wanted to stay longer in Bangkok, I just had to renew my tourist visa. Having a home base made it so that I didn't need to carry my luggage around everywhere I went. It also gave me an idea of the types of day trips and activities that I could participate in when I wasn't working.

Decide What Kind of Trip You Want

When I was researching Thailand, many blogs advised that I go to Chiang Mai or a low-key part of the country. Personally, I didn't care for that kind of lifestyle. I was 23/24. I wanted to be at the center of the party and be able to go to live music and dancing locations!

I also knew that I wanted to be by a beach, because it was super cold in New York City at that time of the year. By simply making note of the items that I cared about and didn't care about, it was easier to narrow down where I wanted to go in the world and which place would give me the most happiness for the time that I was there.

When I visited El Salvador in search of my birth mother, I wasn't planning on doing terribly much work, so I wasn't too concerned about things like WIFI connections. I had to do some things, like answer emails, but I wasn't going to produce very much new content. Therefore, I was more willing to stay in not-so-great accommodations in El Tunco (the surfing town), and trade modern amenities for a more authentic experience.

Write down the items that are important to you for the trip and the level of their importance. This will help you decide on which region of the world you want to go and the best time to go there.

Set Up Safety Nets

I can't say this loud enough. Set up safety nets! You're going to be on the other side of the world. What if something bad happens? What if your passport is stolen? What if your wallet is stolen? What if your laptop dies?

Plan for these unexpected events before they happen!

I made sure to use my room safe at all times, kept spare change, a backup passport photocopy and photos, and made sure that everyone in my area (like my landlord) knew my name and face in case I ever got locked out.

I also backed up my laptop, copied crucial data from my phone, used a waterproof case for my phone when I went into the water, and purchased emergency travel insurance so that I could get back to the USA if I had some kind of medical accident.

I was always very aware of my surroundings, where the exits were for any place I went, and I didn't engage in any conversations when I was interrupted by a local on the street, asking me a question or offering something. As you become a more seasoned traveler, you can take some liberties with this, but for rookies, you'll wanna have your wits about.

Here are a few simple recommendations to set up your safety net:

- Make a photocopy of your passport and email it to yourself or store it in a Dropbox folder.

- Make a monthly backup of your laptop, phone, and any other device you bring with you.

- Bring $200 - $500 in cash as emergency money that you store in a carryon bag.

- Pack your valuables in your carryon bag, in case your suitcase gets lost by the airline

- Take screenshots in your phone of your accommodations (Airbnb, etc), in case you don't have WIFI when you arrive, or you need to write down the address on your tourist card to enter the country.

- Set up a google voice number, in case you need to make a phone call via internet.

- Create a privacy.com account in case your credit cards don't work abroad. Get $5 free:

  (https://www.salvadorbriggman.com/privacy)

- Set up google alerts to stay up to date on news as you travel.

- Bring a basic small medical kit and multi-tool.

- Consider travel insurance

- Email your itinerary to friends and family in case you go missing

- Tell your bank where you're going

Aside from these tips, use your common sense. If you're visiting a foreign country, they may have unique cultural standards when it comes to clothing, especially for women. Be aware of the various political sentiments. It can be illegal, in some countries, to bad mouth the government. Don't be too flashy if you're inebriated. Use your brain.

To date, I've had three times in my travels where I encountered dangerous or potentially dangerous individuals. The first was when I was in Thailand at a bar, and someone tried to snatch the money out of my wallet when I went to open it. I was lucky enough to have grabbed their wrist, and very sternly told them to let go. Eventually, they did. This was dumb on my part. I had been drinking and I had about $100 in the wallet. I should have been more discreet about getting out money.

The second time I was in Colombia walking down the street at night. I was going from my Airbnb, which was in a safe area, to a McDonalds two blocks down the road. The only difference was that the road was on a highway. As I was walking, I took out my white phone to make sure I was headed in the right direction, and at that moment two motorbikes pulled in front of me. They started yelling angrily in Spanish and were pointing at my phone. They were trying to get me to hand it over. I had not yet backed up my phone, and there was lots of critical information on it.

I quickly assessed the situation. They were young kids, maybe 17 – 20, and they were stopped on the side of the road while traffic was roaring past. I made the quick decision that I was going to run back along the sidewalk to my Airbnb, while also flailing my arms at oncoming cars to draw attention. I did that, and because they were faced the wrong way, they couldn't easily circle around to chase me. Eventually, they just gave up and drove off. I felt very lucky and pretty stupid. Physically, I could have taken the kids, but they could have had a hidden knife or a gun.

 The third time, I was in Manila on my way to the rest of the Philippines. This is around when corona virus hit, and things were getting shut down. It was late at night and I was hungry, so I left my apartment, which was in a nice area, and went down the street to 7-11. As I was walking, I noticed two street transgender ladies calling to me. I ignored them, but one came up to me and started to talk. I kept walking, but she was touching my arm/chest and saying how good looking I was. I told her to go away, and she left. Ten seconds later, I felt my pant leg and noticed that my phone was gone.

Thankfully, I had been texting before this encounter, so there was no doubt in my mind that she had stolen my phone. For a second there, I had questioned whether or not I left it in the room. I ran after the transgender girl, grabbed her arm, and threatened her. She said she didn't have the phone. I kept her from moving, threatened her more, and eventually I just told her that I would pay her if she gave the phone to me. I said it was the last chance. She looked at her friend, and then rolled her eyes and took the phone out of her bra. I gave her $5 and she left. This was another example of me not being aware of my surroundings. I am very lucky that I recognized it was her, and that she was still in the immediate area. Otherwise, I would have been out of a thousand-dollar apple phone, along with all of my data.

It's always important to have your guard up, especially at night. Hopefully some of the tips I listed and the stories I shared will remind you of that throughout your travels.

CHAPTER 10: CONCLUSION

You are different from everyone else. You're willing to take risks.

Not many of your friends or family are willing to take a few months off and travel to another country without knowing anyone.

You're slowly coming together with a plan of how it could all work, but it's still risky. It's risky to pick up a new book. It could end up being a waste of your time. It's risky to try working online. You could always fail or need to change your strategy.

I'm going out on a ledge, but I'm willing to bet that you're yearning for something different than your friends and family. You're longing for an adventure. You want to feel alive. You're craving to travel this world and get to know its people. You're tired of browsing through news stories, reading books, or watching YouTube videos of travelers around the world. You now want to be that traveler.

I felt this exact same way.

There is nothing stopping you. You have all of the resources at your disposal. You're smart enough to figure out the income side of the equation. All it takes is research to make a decision on the location and lifestyle components. The only thing holding you back is your own mind.

This reminds me of a time when I was in El Salvador, on a trip to discover whether or not my birth mother was still alive. At this point in my journey, I was visiting a waterfall with a bunch of new friends from a hostel in Santa Ana. I'm going to paste an excerpt of the moment below from my book, Little Thumb of America.

"We're here. Grab your stuff."

I didn't exactly know where "here" was because it looked like we were in the middle of nowhere. On the right, I could see a tiny little house surrounded by a barbed wire fence. Inside the fence, there were chickens walking around. On the left a tiny path led through the trees. I grabbed my backpack and followed the girls down path, filming with my camera.

Jess was telling us about the safety precautions for the cliffs. Her and a guide had scouted out the bottom of the springs to make sure there weren't any jutting rocks. If we wanted to, we were safe to jump off the edge. She'd done it many times before.

The path led into a clearing. I spotted the river. It was snaking towards a precipice not too far off in the distance. A series of rocks poked out of the river, forming a bridge. We hopped from rock to rock to get to the other side, and then started our climb downward towards the base of the waterfall. The rockface was wet and slippery. I made extra effort to brace myself before taking each step.

"Oh my gosh, look at that!" Megan said, as we made our way down the rocks.

In front of us, a full rainbow appeared, nestled between two huge boulders. It was living off the spray from the waterfall. It was majestic. There's no other word for it. It looked like something you'd see out of a movie. The girls quickly took out their phones to snap pictures.

Looking down the river, the water pooled into a series of channels formed by rocks and continued onwards into the distance. When Jess told me about El Salto De Malacatiupan, I was excited to jump off the cliff. After all, I was going be in front of four girls and no way was I going to chicken out. Now that I was at the falls, I wasn't so sure. There were three raging streams shooting off the top cliff, leading into the abyss below. It was a high jump. No doubt about it. I put down my backpack and looked up at the cliff.

"Alright. I'm going!" said Sietse, one of the girls on our trek.

Before waiting for a response, she quickly climbed up to the top of the waterfall and stood defiantly on the edge of the cliff.

"Oh my gosh, this is high." Sietse yelled.

"Wow – that's crazy. I can't do that," said Lauren.

"Yeah, not too sure about that," said Megan.

Jess cupped her hands over her mouth and shouted "Just be sure to push off hard! You'll be fine! You got this!"

We all waited in suspense. Then, she leapt. It was only a few short moments before she hit the water, plunged downwards, and then bobbed back up for air, laughing.

"It's great. Come in!"

I knew if I put it off, I'd never go. What's the worst that could happen? I'd break a leg. Or drown. Heck, life's too short to live out of the now. You gotta seize the moments that come to you, without fear.

While the girls were chatting, I made my way up to the top of the waterfall, making sure to be careful where I stepped. The rocks were slippery and wet. The last thing I wanted was to take a tumble into the vast beyond. I pushed past a bush and reached the edge of the cliff. It was high. Very high.

"Jump! I'll take a video of you!"

"Yeah, jump! Just don't think about it."

As much as I hate to admit it, I don't like being super risky with my health. I came to El Salvador on a mission, but what was the point if I wasn't willing to live life along the way. I was scared, but that's why I had to do it. I had to prove to myself that fear didn't matter anymore. If a girl could do it, then I could.

I closed my eyes and leapt. It felt like an eternity before I hit the water. I remember the feeling of warmth surrounding my entire body. I was confused at first. I expected something chilly and cold. But, the water was warmer than most hot tubs. In fact, it was really nice. I came up for air and paddled towards the side of the river.

"Oh man. It's so warm," I said. "That really surprised me."

Jess smiled. "Yes. You didn't listen so well. These are hot springs."

I laughed and pulled myself up onto a rock. The other girls were laying out sunbathing and taking pictures with their phones. I took a deep breath and looked around. Everything was so clear and sharp. It was warm, beautiful, and tropical. A tropical paradise hidden in a corner of the world that no one visits.

Little did the people living here know that Americans would pay thousands of dollars and travel hundreds of miles to experience a moment like this. To be sprawled out by a waterfall with four beautiful girls in bikinis would be the dream of any man. Here I was living it up in the country that had given birth to me. Why on earth did I leave this place. It is or is as close to being an Eden as I'd ever seen.

"If you want to learn how to become a blogger like me," I said into the camera, "and live a life of freedom, then take a second to check out my book down below, Blogging for Beginners. You're gonna love it. It's on Amazon, Audible, the works. I spent a lot of time and energy sharing my step by step process for starting, launching and monetizing a blog."

I put down the camera and looked around. I was filming in an offshoot to the main spring under the waterfall. It was a tiny spring, almost like a jacuzzi, that oddly enough, had different temperature waters. The river pouring down from the mountain incredibly warm, but at different sections, the sub-streams pouring down the mountain were cooler. I had been filming a video for my YouTube channel, talking about freedom, business, and living the laptop lifestyle.

"Hey, how's the water?" It was Sietse. Later, I would learn that Sietse left a comfy office job as a lawyer to pursue travel, writing, and new adventures. She'd spent most of her life savings hopping from place to place in Central America, learning Spanish, teaching at different schools, and experiencing the culture.

"It's perfect, come on in!" I pulled myself out of the water and rested on a rock, dangling my legs into the hot springs. "This place is incredible right?"

Sietse nodded, dove down into the water, and the resurfaced under the mini waterfall. She sat there, eyes closed, taking the feeling in, meditating. The river rushed across her back, weaving around her and pouring into the hot spring. Water doesn't fight. It flows with you. It moves around you. Through gentle pressure and persistence, it can re-shape rock and landscapes.

For Sietse, this was a spiritual experience. She'd come to El Salvador and started her journey to discover a part of herself that she'd lost in Belgium. I didn't blame her. Every day, in New York City, I see sullen faces, overcast eyes, and hardworking men and women with pained faces falling asleep on the train. We are a city bred on coffee, cigarettes, alcohol, and sex. A city whose stress runs so high that all its inhabitants must work themselves to the bone just to afford space close to the big skyscrapers. Many of us make good salaries and rake in fat paychecks, but it's all spent in the hopes of one day experiencing the tranquility that I was feeling right now. Delayed gratification for gratification that never comes to pass.

"So, I said," putting down my vlogging camera. "What brings you to this country?"

Sietste opened her eyes, paddled over to me, and rested by my rock. She smiled, looked up at me, and said, "Traveling has always been a part of me. On my first solo trip, I went to Hungary and volunteered with kids in an international group. I was scared, but the excitement was bigger. The next year it was Turkey, then many more countries followed," she smiled, looking into the distance. "You're from New

York, right? I remember I spent 10 days in New York City. It was a dream finally come true, but also the first time I felt very alone and homesick."

New York can do that to you. There's the exciting hustle and bustle of the city. Anything can happen once you're in the thick of it all. The opportunity. The connections. Everything feels alive, vibrant, and full of light. But, there's a dark side to the city that never sleeps. Despite so many people and so many cultures, the grey, impersonal city can be very isolating. It can be very lonely. People are very flaky, fake, and full of promises that will go unfulfilled.

Everyone was on this trip for different reasons. Megan was here to be a dirty hippie, flirt with nomadic guys, and take sweet pictures. Lauren wanted to get as far away as she could from England and experience something totally different. Jess and Julio were trying to build a business. Sietse wanted to find herself, her passion, and her purpose. These are just the kind of people that you don't meet anywhere else, I thought, unless you get outside your comfort zone.

"Time to go!" Jess yelled, collecting her things. "Meet back at the car in five minutes!"

Not only were they in a third world country, but they were also girls, white girls, doing crazy stuff like hitchhiking, riding chicken busses, and going where no one else would dare to go. I respected the hell out of them for that. I wish I had that kind of courage, but I had read too many bad news stories. I was here for my own reason, but I hadn't told them much about that. Maybe I would later. I grabbed my backpack, hoisted it over my shoulder, and made my way to the beat-up sedan.

Everyone has their own reasons for traveling. When I wrote Little Thumb of America, I was at the stage in my life where I was discovering my roots. I was adopted at the age of 1 and didn't know very much about life in El Salvador. I was trying to figure out whether or not my birth mother was still alive. Deep down, I had hoped that she was. Then, I'd finally be able to see where I came from.

I hope that for whatever reason you are considering this path of becoming a digital nomad, that you find everything that you seek. If you need someone to help you along the path, you can reach out to me and I'll to my best to share with you the resources that helped me. I'll guide you in any way that I can. Either way, good luck and happy travels!

Salvador Briggman

"I learned many great lessons from my father, not the least of which was that you can fail at what you don't want, so you might as well take a chance on doing what you love." - Jim

Sample Chapter from Blogging for Beginners - Passive Income and The Laptop Lifestyle

New York City had just gotten its first blizzard of the year. Schools closed down. The trains stopped working. ABC's Channel 7 Eyewitness news broadcasted a series of storm warnings, urging commuters to stay inside and keep warm. Walking down the street in midtown Manhattan, you could barely see the outline of the tall buildings amidst the flurry of snowflakes.

When I was younger, I remember loving Winter's first snowfall. It was somehow magical. You'd wake up in the morning and find that everything was covered with a beautiful pristine layer of fresh snow. After rushing downstairs and gobbling up breakfast, you'd bundle up with every piece of clothes you could get your hands on so that you could go out and play.

Where I grew up, there were several epic sledding hills, ice skating ponds, and even a tiny mountain that boasted a handful of skiing trails. It a small suburban town not far from Concord, Massachusetts. For those of you history buffs, that's where the first military engagements of the Revolutionary War took place.

Unfortunately, New York City was a different matter. With so many cabs, tourists, busses, and trains, those clean fluffy snowflakes quickly turn into a brown slushy mixture that coats the entire city. It feels cold, windy, and wet. No one wants to leave their house or commute to work on the subway. When winter hits, it's harsh.

I'd tell you that I was just as miserable as the rest of New York when the blizzard hit, but for the first time in my life, I wasn't. While everyone was groaning about the storm, I was spending those brutal winter weeks relaxing on a beach in Thailand. It was a paradise.

Before leaving the United States, I secured an Airbnb in Phuket, Thailand for the price of $28 per night. This price included daily cleaning, free coffee and snacks, discounts on business in the area, and best of all, I had the entire studio to myself. It was incredible! I couldn't believe it.

Every day, I'd wake up, walk down the street to a café, and spend two hours in the morning working. Usually this consisted of reading new books, journaling, and answering any urgent emails. Then, I'd spend the rest of my time sprawled out on the beach, sipping cold beer, and swimming in the warm water.

When I first arrived, I joined a gym that was a ten-minute walk from my AirBnb so that I could work out each week and stay in shape. I know that might sound crazy, but I really do enjoy lifting weights, seeing muscle gains, and doing cardio. It puts me in such a positive mood. It also is a confidence booster. The gym also had an amazing view looking over the ocean that just made me smile.

At night, there were a ton of options to choose from. If you wanted to party it up, there were tons of bars, clubs, and dance spots to check out. For a more low-key experience, there were also lots of delicious restaurants and live music venues. Lastly, there were neat fire performances on the beach, where you could just sit and listen to the waves or gaze at the stars. It was heaven.

On a more serious note, while I was in Thailand, I also worked on myself a lot. I did yoga, meditation, and spent some quality time outlining my future goals. This "self-care" and "self-examination" work paved the way for the future. It's helped me align my work more closely with my values. I've come to learn more about my natural tendencies and inclinations. In a weird way, it helped me put all of the noise on hold so that I could take some quality time to really find myself.

As I traveled throughout Thailand, I made small talk with many of the locals and other travelers. I formed a few friendships and even began to explore some of the tropical islands in the area with newfound travel buddies. After visiting Phuket, I spent some time in Bangkok and got to see many of the cool temples, neat architecture, and the opulent Grand Palace.

I gotta tell you, I was happier than I had been in a long time. I was having adventures and loving every minute of it. It was a good trip all around.

So, why am I telling you about this? Because, there is only **one reason** that I can travel, work from anywhere, and make money on autopilot. This freedom allows me to live life on my own terms, without having to report to a boss. That reason can be summed up in two words: passive income.

Passive income is defined as money that comes into your pocket **whether or not** you work. You could be sleeping, chilling on a beach in Thailand, or writing a novel, but you'll still be making money. It's what all those scammy infomercials promise and how you'll "make money in your sleep." Never in my wildest dreams did I think that it could ever be a real possibility. It seemed too good to be true, and I didn't trust the people who promised that kind of a lifestyle. There just wasn't something right about them.

The mentality of most entrepreneurs is to make a bunch of money and then retire at age 40. Then, they'll be able to do what they really want. They won't have to spend their time caught in the rat race. They'll **finally** be happy.

This type of thinking can lead to a lot of sacrifices, destroyed relationships, and unhappiness. It can also lead to unethical behavior and the unhealthy willingness to succeed at any cost. As young men and women, we're sold the American dream by venture capitalists and entrepreneurship magazines.

We're told to work insane hours out of the hopes of one day being able to retire rich. Like Budd Fox says in the classic 1987 movie Wall Street,

"I think that if I can make a bundle of cash before I'm thirty and get out of this racket, I'd be able to ride my motorcycle across China."

I'm here to share with you a strategy that will allow you to earn passive income online so that you enjoy your life **now**, not later. Once you set up these systems, you'll be able to decide how you'd like to spend your time. You could decide to continue to grow your income. You could spend your time sunbathing in a tropical climate. You could even spend more time with your family or your kids. It's up to you.

Why Blogging is So Lucrative

Let's be honest. Most bloggers **struggle** to make ends meet. In fact, I'd say that the majority of bloggers are NOT making a full-time income. They're just doing it as a hobby.

There's nothing inherently wrong with that. We all have our own hobbies. I love to fly drones and make vlogs. The weird thing is that when you do some research, you'll quickly discover that a handful of bloggers are absolutely killing it.

They're making a very good living doing what they love.

How can that be?

Why is it that the "rewards" go to a select few?

Why is blogging so lucrative for **them.**

The answer is the same reason why most people have been to a gym in their lifetime, but chances are, they aren't as fit as they'd like to be.

Perseverance and training.

Simply put, most people quit way too soon. They are dabblers. They try out blogging for a month, maybe two, and then go on to other things.

They don't stick with it. There isn't enough time for them to experience the rewards that this career offers.

Wanna hear something crazy?

At the time you are reading these words, I have written over 800 blog posts in my lifetime. With a war chest of 800 pieces of content online, people are continually discovering my website day in and day out. It's almost impossible for me NOT to make money.

I'm not saying you have to write that many articles. Heck, once you start making money, you can pay other people to write the blog posts for you.

All I'm saying is that you need to be willing to persevere if you'd like to earn a substantial amount of income from blogging. I know that's hard to do. It's gonna help if you have an accountability partner.

The second fatal reason that most bloggers fail to earn a full-time income from their craft boils down to one word.

Training.

All of us, myself included, are only as good as our training. Superior results comes from superior education. We all stand on the shoulders of giants who figured out "how things work" and then taught us.

Everything from your computer all the way down to your shoes were created by other people. The only reason they were able to make them for YOU, is because someone taught them how!

Someone else went through all of the headaches, setbacks, and turmoil it takes to figure out a solution. Then, they taught it to someone else. This is the core reason why human beings improve over time. We are able to work off of and add to the findings of our ancestors.

Think about how much money you've spent to get educated.

How many tax dollars went into your education?

How much did you accumulate in student loans?

Education is **expensive** because it's **valuable.**

The bloggers who earn a full-time income from their work deliberately set time aside to master this craft. Just as I did, they sought out mentors and learned how to drive traffic, build an audience, and make money.

You can do the exact same thing.

Are you ready to build a profitable business around YOUR lifestyle?

No more dreadful commutes to work. No more late, stressful, nights slaving away for a boss you can't stand. Finally, you'll be able to work from anywhere, earn dependable passive income, and most importantly, gain a renewed sense of purpose, knowing that you're working on your passion.

In 2012, I was just like you, I had seen the online success stories and was wondering whether or not this was something that I could actually do to earn a healthy income. Late at night, I wondered what it would be like write blog posts for a living.

I could work from wherever I wanted, whenever I wanted.

I could get paid for doing what I loved... writing!

I wouldn't have to put up with an annoying boss and stupid corporate inefficiencies.

Most of all, the promise of making six or even seven figures online was too appealing to ignore. At that time, I had NO IDEA whether or not this blogging thing would really work. I kind of doubted myself, to be honest.

Like... a lot of doubt.

I didn't know anything at all when it came to "online marketing." I had no money to spend on fancy advertisements or any kind of equipment.

But, I did have one thing. I had the desire to do better in my life. For once, I decided that I was going to take action, no matter what happened.

I might be a laughingstock among my friends. I might waste my time on something silly. But, I was going to at least try.

The potential rewards far outweighed the risks!

This is the moment that I went "all-in" and committed myself to becoming a professional full-time blogger. It wasn't easy. There were many failures and stumbling blocks along the way. I learned a lot of difficult lessons.

But, it was all worth it. Two years later in 2014, I finally realized my dream. For the first time in my life, I earned $30,000 from my blog.

I felt like I was rich. It was more money than I had ever made in my life, and what's more, it was all from doing something I loved.

The next year, I earned $50,000.

I started to see more and more people becoming interested in my work. I was cited in many major media publications, like Forbes, CNN, The Wall Street Journal, The New York Times, and more.

I'm happy to share with you that last month I earned more revenue than my entire first year in 2013. Crazy, huh?

Now… you might be thinking… ***well, that's all great for you, Sal, but what about me??***

Oh man. I wish I had a mentor when I was getting started. It would have changed my life. I would have succeeded so much faster.

You know what?! I just wish that I had someone I could trust and that would help me along the path. That's what I really wanted.

As I've become older, I've cared less and less about making money and more about building a legacy. I want to impact the world for the positive.

Today, I'm here to share with you what was NEVER shared with me.

A *step-by-step proven framework* that you can use to start, grow, and monetize your blog.

This is the *exact* process that I used to grow a blog from 0 to more than 20,000 subscribers.

I'm going to reveal the remarkably effective tactics I've used to get more than *2 million visitors* to my website. I'm sharing everything with you. You just have to copy it!

Take note, because this moment is literally going to transform your entire life.

There are a lot of programs online that "teach you how to do things," but I'm not *only* a teacher. I talk the talk and I *walk the walk.*

I was at a networking event last week doing my thing.

I like meeting new peeps. It's hard to make new friends/connections in NYC, so I always try to get out and about.

100% of my customers find me online now, so I just go to these types of events to be social and have fun.

Yes, I'm a nerd.

Anyway, I was talking with this dude about my biz. He seemed cool. He was working on this new social networking startup.

All of a sudden, this older, but beautiful, brunette introduced herself and entered the conversation.

She was tall, lithe, and good looking. She visibly increased the tension in the room. Under any other setting, it would probably be hard to keep eye contact with her.

In the past, this is the kind of girl I would have TOTALLY gone after. Now, I'm happily dating someone. I started to share a bit of what I do, and how I started my own business, when she interrupted me…

"I hear a lot of people say they're entrepreneurs when really, they're just unemployed."

Ouch! Hahah.

Granted, the word "entrepreneur" is thrown around a lot now a days. It's kind of lost its meaning, wouldn't you agree?

I laughed, ignored the comment, and went on to explain how I'm a blogger, etc.

She gave me a weird look… ***"You can make money with that?"***

You'll find that this is a VERY common question.

Mainstream people can't really wrap their head around how you can work from home, make good money, and be your own boss.

I've been full-time as a blogger since 2014. It's nothing new to me. I still find it amusing that people find it socially acceptable to ask "how much do you make?" as a blogger.

In any other context, that question would be considered borderline rude. But, that's a small price to pay for being able to set your own hours, do work that you love, and live a life of tremendous freedom!

Now, you might wanna know how much money you can make so that you can figure out whether or not to spend time on this whole blogging thing. ***Right?***

Before we talk turkey, let me just say that making money from a blog is not something that you do over night. It takes time, consistent work, and a lot of learning.

For me, it took a year before I was able to go full-time on my first professional blog. In that year, I made ~$30k. The year after, I made $50k. It's been an upward climb since then!

My Initial Sources of Income:

- **Adsense:** This is Google's advertising program. You can put banner ads on your website and make money.

- **Consulting:** I was making money by offering consulting services.

- **Services**: I was offering a business service to my readers, which generated income.

This first year, I also wrote an ebook that I sold on my own website, but it didn't make a tremendous amount of money. It takes quality traffic to make good money from advertisements or affiliate marketing. It also takes knowledge and time to put together digital products.

Therefore, when you start out, your primary source of income is going to come from services or consulting. You'll be trading time for money.

Can You Make Money Directly From Blogging?

Since a blog is free, the simple answer is no. The free content that you put out is meant to develop a relationship with a particular type of reader.

Once that reader is on your website, you can monetize their attention in a variety of ways. For the most part, this includes advertisements, sponsored content, digital products, services, and affiliate marketing.

<u>**How Much Can You Actually Make?**</u>

The top bloggers don't really consider themselves to be bloggers. They're content marketers. As I've shared before, they use the blog to attract 'leads' and monetize those leads by selling them digital courses and products.

Now, of course there are fashion and entertainment bloggers out there that aren't selling these types of products. However, they're selling *other people's* products in the form of sponsorships advertising, and affiliate marketing,

At a certain point, a "professional blogger" might decide to use their excess funds to hire a team and turn their online presence into an education company or an entertainment company.

All of this being said, as an individual blogger, you can probably expect the upper tiers to make $100k – $200k max with *a lot of hard work* over a span of *5-10 years*.

This income is likely not solely derived from blogging. It probably also comes from services, products, affiliate marketing, etc. You can certainly make more than this, but at this stage, you're transitioning more into an internet marketer and using things like webinars to sell high ticket products.

A more *realistic goal* is to make between $30k – $80k, depending on how hard you're willing to work and the breakdown between selling services vs. other forms of monetization. Your niche also plays a big role.

Overall, the majority of bloggers don't make very much money at all. It's more of a hobby for them. If you want to make money, you gotta treat it like a business.

<u>**What would YOUR life be like if...:**</u>

- You never had to report to a boss EVER AGAIN.

- You never had to commute to work in the rain, snow, and cold.

- You could work **whenever** you want, **wherever** you want (even if that's from a beach in Thailand).

- You could spend more time with your family, friends, and wife or girlfriend.

- You could FINALLY earn $30k, $50k, or $80k per year doing something that you love.

Imagine how it would feel to be able to wake up at a reasonable time, make a healthy breakfast, and check out a cool cafe in your area.

The cafe has a friendly staff and maybe one or two other professional types are working there with their laptops. They're banging away at their keyboard.

You order a drink and a snack and then sit down at a table close to the window. It's peaceful. Every once in a while, you can see some pedestrians walking past the cafe. You pull out your laptop and get to work.

You're there, sipping a steaming cup of coffee or tea, and working on a new blog article for next week. As you type on the keyboard, your mind is racing. You have so many ideas that are just flowing through your fingertips. You already know, this is gonna be a killer post!

How freakin' great would it feel to be able to say that was YOUR day?

Pretty epic, right?

Well now it can be...

<u>Let me introduce you to a career with:</u>

- **Job stability:** It will take some time to get set it all up, but once you do, you can't be fired. You are the boss!

- **Unlimited income potential:** You can make a much or as little as you'd like. Once you're earning $30k, $50k, or $80k per year, you can sit back and relax. Or, you can work to continue to earn even more money. It's up to you.

- **Passive income opportunities:** Visitors can stumble on your website without you having to be there. This allows you to earn money in your sleep. Your time won't be tied to your income.

- **Influence and authority:** In a small way, you can be famous! People will know who you are, without ever having met you in person. This makes you feel powerful and influential. Just don't let it go to your head.

- **Location-independence:** You can work from home, a cafe, or anywhere else. You don't have to report to an office location every day. You can spend your free time as you like.

All you gotta to do get started is **educate yourself!** And... you're doing that right now! Every worthwhile income-earning opportunity in life has required this.

If you want to become an accountant, you gotta go through 12 years of school and then 4-8 years of college and post-graduate work.

Not to mention that now a days the average cost of college is *$34,000* for private institutions and *$9,970* for in-state residents attending public colleges.

That isn't in total... that's PER YEAR.

This doesn't include other fees, special housing, or food.

Over four years, that's $136,000 that you'll be paying for the opportunity to earn a job that starts at *MAYBE $30k – $50k.*

The funny thing is that if you want to earn more, you'll have to then pay for even more schooling, am I right? You can earn the SAME amount of income from the comfort of your home and it doesn't cost $136,000 to do it.

In this book, you will discover how to become a full-time blogger for a fraction of the cost.

The Real Benefit of Blogging

This can be summed up in one word… **FREEDOM!**

Just imagine how awesome it would be to be your own boss. You don't have to commute to work every day. You can work from home, a cafe, a beach in a foreign country, or really, **anywhere** you want.

I've worked from a lot of different locations including:

- Co-working spaces in Manhattan
- Cafes in Brooklyn
- Other countries (Thailand, Cuba, etc)

Since you run your own life, you can also decide **when** you work. You don't have to wake up early if you don't want to.

Pretty cool, eh?

So… is blogging dead?

Not at all. The "heyday" of blogging was about 2005 – 2009. I started mine in late 2012. I **made $30k** when I went full-time about a year later. I think that most people see the popularity of online video and social media platforms and they assume that people don't read blogs any more.

This is 100% false. There are some factors that have changed in the blogging industry, most notably comments and SEO, but it's not going anywhere.

You can still start a blog today and be VERY successful. In the next chapter, I'm going to show you step-by-step how to start a professional blog quickly. I'll walk you through what you need to do to get started and be with you ever step of the way. Now that you have an idea of how much you can earn, it's finally time to get started!

If you enjoyed this expert, you can read the rest in the book "Blogging for Beginners: Work from Home, Travel the World, Provide for Your Family by Salvador Briggman". It is available as a paperback, ebook, and Audible book. I hope that you enjoy it, and if you do, please leave a good Amazon review. Thank you!

Sal

ABOUT THE AUTHOR

Salvador Briggman founded the popular blog, CrowdCrux, which has been cited by the New York Times, The Wallstreet Journal, CNN, and more. He helps entrepreneurs raise money on crowdfunding platforms like Kickstarter and Indiegogo. Last year, he helped nearly 400,000 individuals raise money from the crowd through his website, products, newsletter, and forum.

<u>Other Relevant Books that Salvador has Written:</u>

- **Blogging for Beginners:** Work from Home, Travel the World, Provide for Your Family

- **Podcasting for Beginners:** Podcasting for Beginners: Start, Grow and Monetize Your Podcast

- **Unlocking Human Potential:** How to Raise Your Consciousness Step-by-Step

- **Little Thumb of America:** Searching For My Birth Mother in El Salvador

- **Kickstarter Launch Formula:** The Crowdfunding Handbook for Startups, Filmmakers, and Independent Creators.